Voiceless

Marie McCreadie

Prologue

The bathroom mirrors swim one way and the other. The fluorescent tubes stamp shafts of light through my head. My heart is pounding and the tickle at the back of my throat turns into searing pins and needles as I throw up. Everything becomes superimposed. The smell of disinfectant, the vomit, the sounds of the office through the door; everything becomes one thing – a wave of pain.

As I struggle to keep it together, the song between my ears grows louder. One line, "where seldom is heard a discouraging word", loops around and around like a proverbial broken record. I don't even like country music, for heaven's sake. Why can't it be an Elvis track or maybe Cliff Richard stuck in my head?

I want to scream, but of course I can't make a sound. At this time, in my mid-twenties, I've been mute for half my life. Since childhood, every one of my experiences has been more or less shaped by the loss of my voice. It's been so long since I was able to speak that I can't really remember what it was like.

Repressed moments of trauma flicker through my mind as I try to stop myself throwing up again. Darren, my first fiancé, laughing with his mates as he humiliates me. Eric, my friend in the psychiatric ward, lying unconscious, his red cap fallen to the floor tiles below. Morgan, from the coven, inviting me to that fateful 'get together', to be among "people who understand you". The lyrics in my head lose themselves in distortion: "Where never is heard a single word… where never is heard a single word…"

I replay my vision of Terry, my cousin, blown to bits by an IRA bomb. I picture my friend Kim, decapitated and fingerless, dumped on Jamberoo Mountain. The distillations pile up on each other as the floor heaves at my feet and the mirrors buckle in towards me. The image of a swarm of maggots in a dog's bowl comes out of nowhere. I flail out and somehow manage to cling to the basin that keeps shifting in front of me.

Every breath feels like fire. I close my eyes and hold on for dear life.

The nausea and the pain bring back physical memories from my last day at school, all to the surreal soundtrack of 'Home on the Range'. I can hear Father Moran screeching at me as I cling to the edge of the basin. I can almost feel him ripping me away; dragging me by the hair out of the bathroom and into St John's Church. I can smell fear in the vomit on my clothes.

I am somewhere on the verge of passing out. It's like when I overdosed on those little white pills, only much more visceral and intense. Instead of gentle clouds and snippets of my favourite songs floating by, it feels as if I am being stabbed by shafts of light; as if I am being deafened by the noise in my head. It feels as if my insides are being torn out of me.

I retch again and feel something tearing at the back of my throat. I try to swallow but it's like barbed wire. I hear a strange rasping sound and I taste blood. I don't know what's going on. Am I dying? Is God punishing me for my sins?

Chapter 1

Looking back now, I don't know how I got through it all. All I know is that I carried on. I had to, that was the way I was brought up. "Crying won't help anything," Nana used to tell me. "If you have to cry," she would say, "go outside, get it over with, and then come back in and carry on with life. That's what you have to do to survive." I guess Nana didn't know how hard things were going to be when she counselled me. But then again, maybe she did...

Nana was born at the turn of the twentieth century in Bolton, a northern English industrial town near Manchester.

In those days, electricity was not yet a thing – the streetlights were still running on gas. Every evening a man would light them with a burning torch cupped on the end of a long staff, and each morning he would return to put them out. As he did this he would knock on the windows with his long staff, waking the men for the day's work.

Nana's father Charlie was a 'barrow boy'. Each morning, when the gas man knocked, he would pull on his clothes - a heavy coat, woollen mittens and wooden clogs – and head out onto the streets. The only traffic in those days were horses and carts and barrows like the one Charlie had. Charlie would pick up his vegetables and fruit (when fruit was available) from local farmers, and he would park his barrow alongside the others in the town square, ready to sell. The days were long and Charlie's voice, by Nana's account, was permanently hoarse from all the years of calling out his wares.

Like most of the women in her family, Nana left school young. She was needed at home to help with the washing and cooking, and she worked in the cotton mills from the age of twelve, except for during World War 1, when manufacturing ammunitions was more important. Nana was a woman of her time and place. She would always insist that English cotton was the best. "Won't have none of that foreign stuff," she'd say.

Manchester and its surrounding towns were ideal locations for mills in the old days, because the rivers that raced down from the Pennine Hills provided a constant power supply. The damp air also prevented the cotton threads from snapping too often. Bolton had already been an industrial centre for over a hundred years, but Nana lived at a time when Britain's cotton industry peaked – eight billion yards of cloth was produced the year she started working. The growth of the textile industry had been boosted by steam power and of course the coal mines in and around Bolton. One of the most serious coal mining disasters in history was at the Pretoria Pit on 21st December 1910, when 344 men and boys were killed in an explosion.

With all the concrete and the brick walls of the factories and the grimy cobblestone streets, it was as if there was no room in Bolton for trees or plants or green grass. The sun was a rare visitor and the days almost always seemed to be grey and overcast. Even when it wasn't raining it was dreary and cold - a wet, damp, icy cold that seeped into your bones.

Nana's family lived on the low-income side of town, in an old terraced house with two bedrooms upstairs and the kitchen and lounge room downstairs. There was no bathroom, just an outside toilet down the backyard. In winter Nana would run the eight or nine steps to the end of the yard over wet and slippery flagstones that were often covered in snow. Toilet paper was unheard of - old newspapers would be ripped into squares and left on a hook on the wall. High fences divided the yards from each other but the ladies could all be seen on Mondays, scrubbing their front steps with a donkey stone to keep them white and looking nice. Despite the hardships there was still pride in keeping a tidy home.

Nana's mother died after giving birth to her youngest brother, and as Nana was the eldest it was left up to her to look after all the other children. It was a hard life and she grew up fast, but she was spellbound when she first saw her husband, Lawrence O'Toole, at church. "Oh Marie, he was so handsome, with his top hat and cane," she told me. She was smitten, but everyone warned her that it wouldn't work. Sure enough, a few years after they married Lawrence left her for other women (as in more than one). His family had never approved of Nana - apparently she was 'below their station'. I don't think Lawrence ever found a woman that matched his station. He eventually died from war injuries, but he was already dead to Nana long before that.

Nana wanted better for herself and her family. She taught herself to read and write as a mature woman, and she started nursing during the second World War, by which time she had five children of her own as well as three siblings and Charlie, her father, living with her.

Veronica O'Toole, my mum, was the youngest of Nana's children. She did well at school and wanted to continue her education after she turned fifteen, but in the 1940's that didn't happen unless you had money. So Mum started a 'career' in Bolton's cotton mills, like Nana before her.

The nearby city of Manchester is still synonymous with sheets and bedding, and when most people think of cotton they imagine a clean natural material, but Mum had bad skin like most of the ladies in the cotton mills. Dust mites, sweat and dirt all played a part. It was noisy and dirty work. Lacking bathrooms at home, Mum and her workmates would go to the public baths on Friday nights before going out dancing on Saturdays.

Mum's sister Mary also worked at the cotton mill. One day Mary's hair worked itself loose and got caught in one of the machines. They couldn't stop it quickly enough and she was scalped, losing all of her hair and the skin on her head. There were quite a few accidents like that in those days, so Mum was greatly relieved when the girls were finally allowed to wear pants (trousers) at work. They had fewer mishaps in pants than they did with their skirts flapping about and getting caught, and it was also more comfortable when she was riding her bicycle home.

Mum and Dad met at Burt Mayo's Ballroom Dancing classes when they were both nineteen years old. Mum was short like me and Dad was 6ft tall, but when they danced they just looked good together. Mum used to wear a pink and black taffeta dress. I remember watching her dance in that dress when I was little, and thinking how beautiful she looked.

In 1957 Mum and Dad were married in St Patrick's Church in Bolton. They applied to immigrate to Australia just after they were married, but then Mum became pregnant and they put their plans on hold so that she could have me and then my little sister Denise with family around.

Looking back on it, Dad just wanted a better life for us - he and Nana had that in common. When he was laid off work Mum returned to the mills so they could put food on the table, but they didn't want their daughters to end up there too and they didn't like the way England was going. The politics of the day were not in our favour and we didn't have Social Security benefits then. Australia was Nana's idea - she told us about Mum's distant cousins that had moved to New South Wales in the 1950s. She was always showing us the postcards, talking about opportunity. I thought the postcards looked nothing like Wales - the beaches seemed to go on forever in Australia.

In those days the 'Troubles' were brewing in Northern Ireland. I remember being on holiday in Ireland in 1968 and having to leave quickly as places nearby were bombed. Trouble was also brewing closer to home with the family next door. One day Dad went over and there was an argument. They told him that King George had attacked their baby. King George was my six-week-old puppy. He loved licking everyone's feet and he wouldn't hurt a flea. We kept him in the yard, but Mum told me that he had disappeared that morning while I was at school. That's why Dad had gone over to our neighbour's house, looking for him.

The policeman who came to our house had a thick moustache and his breath smelled of onions. He told me they had taken my dog to live on a farm where he would be happy, but I knew he was lying because Dad had found King George's body around the corner. I heard Dad tell the policeman that he'd seen dogs that had been run over and he'd seen dogs beaten to death before. He said he knew the difference. Dad sounded strange. I think he was crying.

But the policeman said there was no evidence. He said if Dad complained about the neighbours he would be labelled a racist. That night Mum told me that King George was in puppy heaven. I asked her why the family next door were so angry. She told me that their religion forbade them from touching dogs, or else they had to wash themselves seven times. I know it must have been hard for them, moving to a strange new country but I also remember the human excrement that was thrown over the wall into our yard the next day. King George was already dead. That family just wanted us out of the neighbourhood.

Around that time Nana received another postcard from Australia. So I guess this prompted Dad to look into it again. It was 1970 - a new decade and time for a fresh start. Eventually they received a letter from the Australian Embassy with a date for emigration: 7 February 1971.

I knew something was going on, but I wasn't sure what it meant. Children were not involved in family decisions in those days and we weren't meant to ask questions. Denise and I were just told we were moving to Australia. But I remember friends and relatives being dumbfounded. "Why would you do that?" they asked. "Don't you know it's on the other side of the world?"

Up until then my life had felt very ordinary. I'd started school at St Peter and Paul's aged 4, and every Sunday after church we would go to Nana's for dinner with my cousins and aunts and uncles. The adults would sit in the lounge room and watch a movie while the kids would play. We made a cubby house under the stairs and would dress up in old curtains. Sometimes my cousin Ann and I would play 'Robin Hood' and chase Michael around the neighbourhood with our homemade bows and arrows. Poor Michael couldn't understand why he had to die all the time when the men on TV were always the heroes.

I also spent a lot of time at my Aunt Mary's, and when we were supposed to be outside playing, my cousin Paul and I would hide behind the couch in the living room and read his comics..

We were a close family, and I didn't realise how much I would miss everyone until we were half a world away. Before we left us kids didn't really know what the problem was. Why were the adults so upset? Sure, we'd see each other again - Australia couldn't be *that* far away. We'd just have to get a few more buses or maybe a train, right?

Of course I didn't know anything about Australia then. None of us did. So I watched 'Skippy' on TV every afternoon, to see where we were going. It looked great, kangaroos jumping around everywhere, and no school. They used a CB radio to attend class. How much fun would that be!

The Australian government arranged for Dad to have a job as soon as we arrived. Dad was an insulation engineer so he was to be employed by the steelworks at Port Kembla in Wollongong. Everything seemed to happen very quickly. A couple of weeks later we visited Australia House in London, where we were given various injections and were told about life in Australia by a man in a brown suit. He said that when we arrived we would be taken to stay at a hostel until we were in a position to rent or buy a property.

Oh, and we were expected to attend English lessons. Excuse me? What language did they speak down there?

The man in the brown suit went into great detail about how to live in Australia. He said the worse thing we could do was to 'whinge'. "Whinging poms are the bane of Australia," he said. I thought his voice was strange; hard to understand. There seemed to be too many eees in every sentence. Who was he to talk about English lessons? Anyway, he said we had to stay in Australia for at least three years. We could not leave the country in that time.

The man said we should make friends as soon as we could. "Join a club or sporting facility," he suggested. Us kids were to start school five days after arriving. And Mum was advised to join a church society or to help out in the school so she could meet locals and settle in more quickly. We were warned about 'homesickness' and given recommendations on how to not let it get us down. The man in the brown suit went on and on and on and I stopped listening after a while. I'd heard enough and just wanted to get going. Finally, at the end of the interview, he shook Dad's hand and it was settled.

In February 1971 we left Bolton, the town that had always been home to my family. The furniture and our toys and clothes had already been packed up in tea chests to be shipped to Australia so we stayed with Nana for the last few weeks. A lot of our other stuff had to be sold as we couldn't take everything with us, but Dad didn't need to find a buyer for our house as it turned out that our whole block had been listed for demolition anyway. In the end he was given 200 pounds and that was that.

The day we left, the rooftops were covered in snow. The cobblestones were slippery and covered in a dirty grey mush that slid underneath my feet as I walked. I remember wearing socks in a plastic covering, and then more socks inside my wellies, to keep my feet from getting wet. There was a big gathering where we said goodbye to all our aunts and uncles and cousins. I remember Mum and her sister Mary crying, and the men making jokes and slapping Dad on the back.

I suddenly remembered the night before when me and Glenys Hurst, my best friend, went to Nancy's Corner Shop and bought a 1p cola ice lolly and a packet of cheese and onion crisps and walked around the streets, something we used to do regularly. Glenys gave me a necklace with the Endeavour on it; she said "It's the ship that Captain Cook sailed to Australia, so it must be lucky." We looked at each other sadly, and she said "Don't worry, we'll see each other again, wait and see." But the way the adults were carrying on, I wasn't so sure.

At the last moment Nana took me aside. "You won't see me again, so remember everything you can about our side of the world, because you won't see anything like it where you're going," she told me. Then I had to kiss her goodbye. She was my grandma, but she had hard sticky skin and worse, she smelled like mothballs. "You're going to paradise," she said as we turned to leave, "even if it is at the bottom of the earth and closer to hell."

Chapter 2

'The Carnival is Over' by the Seekers; that song was played at the school dance, shortly before I left the UK. In the early 1970s the Seekers were one of the most popular bands around, and as a pre-teen girl newly in Australia that song reminded me of all my cousins and friends I had left behind. It made me sad every time I heard Judith Durham sing "I will love you till I die..."

Back in Bolton our family always sang when we got together. Christmas, Easter, football finals - any excuse and we would raise the roof with song. We were so loud that Mum said the neighbours couldn't hear themselves think. Sometimes they would come and join in, just so they wouldn't have to fight against the noise. If you can't beat 'em, join 'em, they must have thought. Anyway, I guess music and singing were in my genes.

Mum bought me a transistor radio shortly after we settled in Australia. I thought it was the best present ever but I think she may have regretted it herself, because from that moment on the radio was constantly stuck to my ear, everywhere I went. I was in heaven. The records that I already had were mainly old ones - Elvis Presley, Cliff Richard, Mario Lanza, Shirley Bassey and the like, and Mum would always be singing or humming around the house, so I knew a lot of musicals from her. But now, with the radio, I could listen to all the shiny new pop idols of the day. 'Chirpy Chirpy Cheep Cheep' was climbing up the charts at the time. It was a song by a Scottish band called Middle of the Road. Terrible name, but what a catchy tune - I guess that's why it sold more than ten million copies around the world.

I could almost hear my cousin Christine's excitement when she wrote to me about it. 'Do you have this song in Australia?' she asked. 'It's number one over here!' 'Of course we have it,' I wrote back to her. 'We're still on the same planet, you know.'

Despite missing family and friends in Bolton, I was enamoured with our new home and I loved living in Shellharbour. Sure, school wasn't quite as fun as I had imagined from watching 'Skippy', but in comparison to England, life in Australia really did feel like paradise to me, just as Nana had described it. It wasn't such a holiday for my parents, however. They worked long hours to make ends meet. Dad left for the steelworks at 6am, six days a week, and Mum got a job at the Shellharbour pub, working from before breakfast until after dinner.

Shortly after we arrived in Shellharbour, the Workers' Club held their annual 'Picnic Day' on the beach. There was free ice cream, chips and lollies for the children so I thought it was the best thing ever, but I couldn't swim and I was wary of the ocean. I ran around on a sugar high like all the other kids, of course - I just didn't follow them into the surf.

We didn't live near the sea back in England but I can remember having nightmares when I was little, where I was drowning, going down into the darkness, trying to hold my breath. I used to bend my legs up under my chin and wrap my arms around them. A voice in my head would tell me to stretch out and let go but then I would wake up, breathless and crying. I don't know where these nightmares came from - maybe I was on the Titanic in a former life?

Anyway, one girl at the picnic told me about a shark attack that had taken place at Coledale, just north of Wollongong. A thirteen-year-old boy had his leg bitten while he was surfing, she said. The way she told it, the shark wouldn't let go, even when they rushed the boy to hospital in the back of a panel van. He was lucky to have survived. The girl probably exaggerated the story but after listening to her I was sure the coast was teeming with killer sharks, just itching to sink their razor-sharp teeth into me.

It was never confirmed as a shark attack but I was at Shellharbour beach on 30 January 1972 when two of my friends went missing. They were sisters, Anne and Heather McBain, aged ten and eight. One minute the girls were there, and the next minute there was a fracas and they were gone. Their brother David rushed into the water but couldn't find them. Mum and Dad were at the Workers' Club when the police came and broke the news to the parents of the children. Everyone was in shock. It was a terrible time for everyone in Shellharbour. Anne's body was recovered intact but nothing was found of Heather until a couple of years later when a jawbone was washed up in Warilla. A DNA match was finally confirmed in 2010.

I know now that sharks get a bad rap, but as an impressionable young girl they only compounded my fear of the ocean. That's why I never learned how to swim properly, despite living in a beach paradise. I tried swimming lessons at the pool a few times, but it always ended up the same - I would be fine until I had nothing to hold onto and then I would panic. I'd hear a roar like the sound you hear when you put a seashell up to your ears, and I would imagine teeth so sharp I could barely feel them, slicing into my body. Soon I'd be completely disorientated, gasping for breath and coughing up water. On more than one occasion I had to lie down at the side of the pool to recover.

One weekend we were invited to the house of a new friend of Dad's for a 'barbie'. "It's Australian for BBQ," Dad explained, as if he wasn't as confused as the rest of us. Call it what you will, we hadn't been to a barbeque before. "They said to bring a plate," Dad added, so Mum thought the poor things must be short on crockery. We took not just one plate but four - one for each of us. Little did we know that in Australian culture 'bring a plate' means 'with food on it'.

As a child I was a big fan of Hayley Mills - I watched her films on the TV show 'Disneyland'. It wasn't new at the time, but the first movie I saw in Australia was one of Hayley's called 'In Search of the Castaways', co-starring

Michael Anderson. I think it was based on an old Jules Verne novel. As the movie ends they are on a ship, just escaped from an island full of 'savages', and he takes her out on the deck to show her the Southern Cross. Then, as she turns back to face him, he kisses her on the lips.

At that time I had a huge crush on Kurt Russell. In my pre-teen brain I fantasised about a kiss like that, and since the Southern Cross was so clear in the Australian night sky, I figured I was in the right country for it to happen. So, as young people do, I rewrote the script for 'In Search of the Castaways' with a few changes: my version of the film was set on safe dry land and starred Kurt Russell, turning to kiss *me* under the Southern Cross.

Over those first two years in Shellharbour I practiced speaking what Australians call English and I began to 'fit in'. Then, at the start of 1973, I started high school.

High school is without doubt one of the biggest challenges in a young person's life. It's a time of raging hormones, high politics, and grand angst. My high school years were definitely worse than most, but not knowing what lay ahead, I was excited the day I started at St Anne's Ladies College in Dapto. I had great expectations of close friendships and great adventure and I'd seen enough American movies about high school to believe it was going to be amazing...

St Anne's was a small Catholic school. There were only four classrooms, a library and a science 'lab'. Religious education was the core subject of our curriculum. But had a really cool uniform - a royal blue shift dress over a white shirt (short sleeves for summer, long for winter), with a maroon tie and beret and gloves, and a matching blazer, and because we were all grown up we had to wear stockings (or panty hose if you like).

I only knew two other girls that were starting at St Anne's, but I made friends quickly and was soon part of a tight-knit group: Mary-Kay, Cassandra, Courtney, Marusia, Darlene, Louise and myself. The seven of us came together naturally and got on very well, sharing our daily troubles and our dreams for the future. We all loved rock and roll music and could spend hours swaying with imaginary microphones as we sung along with Elvis Presley, Cliff Richard, David Cassidy, Donny Osmond and the Jackson Five, to hordes of imaginary fans.

Pop songs were a language of our own. We didn't always agree on everything but we all loved Elvis - hence we called ourselves the Elvis group. At the time Elvis had recently separated from his wife Priscilla, and the song 'Burning Love' was on high rotation on the radio. There were probably millions of teenage girls around the world who dreamed of taking Priscilla's place at Graceland, including us. We all felt we were as one with him, like the sweet song of a choir, lit like the morning sky… Until that annoying bell rang for class.

Sister Kathryn was my room teacher in my first year at St Anne's. She was small and wizened and reminded me of an angry little bird. She loved opening windows on cold winter mornings and telling us to suffer the cold. "It will do you good," she would trill, "to suffer like the saints did." My fingers would be so cold I could hardly move them, even when I wore the maroon gloves. I could see my breath when I breathed out. Courtney and Cassandra got into trouble for pretending to smoke.

In summer it was even worse, of course. The heat was relentless in Dapto and there was no air conditioning at the school. Beads of perspiration would trickle down my back and chest and sometimes I couldn't see properly because of the sweat dripping into my eyes. And what did Sister Kathryn say, all the while? "Think of the saints that suffered for us," she said, her eyes turning up toward heaven. "Think of the martyrs that were burned." She drove us crazy with her sanctimony. I didn't really care what the saints had done. Anyway, that's why they were saints - they were goody goodies.

St Anne's school counsellor was a rotund woman with a permanent frown on her face. I didn't yet know that she would become my arch enemy, but Sister St Patrick, as she was called, thought she knew everything we were thinking and would ever think. She assumed that all young girls were preoccupied with sex and boys, and she acted accordingly. Sure, we talked a lot, but believe me, at thirteen we only *pretended* to know about sex and boys. We might have fantasised about kissing, but we didn't really know what we were supposed to *do* after that. And the local boys in Dapto weren't exactly our thing anyway. There were no pop star lookalikes, so there was nothing to worry about there.

In any case, we weren't allowed to talk to boys. If we were seen talking to boys down town we would be punished the next day. "Never let them get to you," Sister St Patrick would caution us. She advised us to imagine something really sickening, something that we hated.

Then, if a boy tried to kiss us, we were supposed to remember that image. All the other girls chose things like sweaty socks or Brussels sprouts. I chose Mick Jagger. Thinking of those huge rubber lips on mine, swallowing me, just left me cold. Mick Jagger has done me well over the years, whenever I've wanted to avoid trouble - that image still works today.

Magazines were contraband at St Anne's. We became clandestine experts at slipping each other the latest 'Tiger Beat' or 'Dolly', or maybe a copy of 'Jackie' that my cousin Christine sent from England. There was nothing particularly risqué about these magazines but the nuns didn't like us learning about 'women's stuff', as they said it would only tempt us to evil things. Of course we wanted to know what these 'evil things' were and *why* they were evil. So when Louise smuggled in a copy of Cosmopolitan with Burt Reynolds posing nude, we were intrigued, even if he wasn't our thing. Maybe we wouldn't have been so interested if the sisters hadn't drawn so much attention to the subject?

If the lack of magazines at St Anne's was restrictive, the lack of mirrors in the toilets was just weird. But mirrors apparently encouraged the sin of vanity, so that's how it was. We were told to wash and complete our toilette as quickly as possible and not to 'touch' ourselves unnecessarily. Huh? Why would we want to do that?

Father Moran was the school priest and head of the local parish of St John's. I suppose he may have been a good man once but by the time we got to him, well, let's just say I don't think he liked his job much. Or teenage girls for that matter. Father Moran was a lanky man with short dark hair and thick black rimmed glasses. He wore a black frock coat which made him look quite morbid, and he liked to serve tennis balls at us as we walked around the school during recess or lunch time. He also used to hit us around the head with his tennis racquet for no other reason than he 'thought' we might have said something insolent.

Father Moran's offsider was the sweet-natured Father Carr. I know he tried his best to smooth things over for us when there was trouble, but his hands were tied as he was only just out of the seminary, and as such was bound to the role of the obedient young apprentice. Even our headmistress, Sister Gerard, answered to Father Moran. Back then the priest was the lord and master of the school - his word was final.

As a student I liked English, science, and history classes but I wasn't too keen on maths or geography. Needlework class was a reprieve from studying and I liked the pretty things I could make. I excelled at embroidery; I had an eye for fine stitching and I found it relaxing, but I didn't like machine sewing - not since I sewed my finger to a dress I was working on. All in all I wasn't a bad pupil except for in physical education, where it was an effort to keep on finding excuses not to participate. I should have at least been awarded top grades for my imagination in that department.

Because we were 'ladies' the girls at St Anne's had to wear stockings, which always had ladders running everywhere. The running joke in our group was to ask "who's climbing your ladder today?" Everyone of us had a favourite, and it was usually David Cassidy climbing mine. Mary-Kay always wanted Elvis so I decided she could have him, even though he was cool, because he was a bit too old for me. Marusia fancied Donny Osmond. She had a poster of him on her wall in her bedroom. One afternoon we were playing records when her mum came in. She took one look at Donny and in her broad Scottish accent she asked "Och, who's that pretty wee lassie?" Marusia was horrified but I thought it was hilarious.

Chapter 3

Have you ever lost your voice? It's frustrating, right? A few days of pointing and nodding and shaking your head, and maybe a hoarse whisper as you recover; that's the usual scenario. People smile sympathetically as you do your best to mouth the words you want to say - everyone's experienced it. Well, my case wasn't like that; I literally couldn't make any sound at all. I couldn't talk, I couldn't ask questions or hold a conversation, and maybe worst of all, I couldn't sing.

After only a couple of months at high school, during the Easter break, it happened. At first all I knew was that I wasn't feeling well. I was thirteen years old and I remember being annoyed that it happened in the holidays, rather than during the school term. Anyway, it started with a sore throat but it got steadily worse, and soon I had a high temperature and I couldn't breathe properly.

I was too sick to go into the surgery so our GP, Dr Michaels, came to our house. "Where's your mum?" he asked. I used his notepad and pen: "She's at the pub," I wrote. I guess I didn't explain that she was actually working there because Dr Michaels raised an eyebrow. "Hmmm," he said, with that tone of disapproval that doctors seem to be so good at. After poking and prodding me he diagnosed me with bronchitis, gave me an injection and said I needed to stay in bed. "Just rest and gargle with salt water," he said. "It should clear up in a day or two."

So I rested and rested, and I gargled with salt water, but I didn't get better. Dr Michaels came back twice a day to give me injections, but that didn't seem to help either, and after a while I came to resent him. It probably wasn't true but I became convinced that he enjoyed pushing that needle in as slowly as possible.

Of course I respected the religious aspects of the holiday, but like most children I mainly loved Easter because of the chocolates. Yes, I knew that Jesus died for our sins so we could all join him in Heaven, but he did it every year, didn't he? It was the chocolates I was worried about as I lay in bed, day after day. In the end I was sick for several weeks, but somehow there were still Easter eggs on the sideboard waiting for me when I got better. I thought it was a miracle.

It was only after I finished the chocolates that it really sunk in. The fever and the pain had passed but I was still completely mute - unable to whisper, squeal, grumble, moan, sing or laugh aloud. I could click my tongue or smack my lips but that was all - my voice had simply not returned with my health. I couldn't utter a sound. I was dumb, in the biblical sense of the word. I had literally lost my voice.

Every now and then I had a sort of hiccup in my throat, but when I tried to force it nothing came out. I was worried and apprehensive and I knew my mother was concerned too, even though she didn't say so. It was so strange - no sound, no sensation, just nothing at all.

I tried everything I could think of. I drank gallons of water. I stood upside down against the end of my bed. I hyperventilated. I pulled the Bible out of my undies drawer and begged God for help. I hailed Mary and recited the Lord's Prayer over and over in my head, but none of it made any difference. I was completely and utterly voiceless.

Tension grew high at home, because no one really knew what was going on. Neighbours were starting to talk about me too. I could hear them whispering when I went to the shops, or when I saw them in the street. A few family friends came around to talk to Mum and ask after me, but not many, and not often. I felt like a freak, slowly withdrawing from situations that involved talking to people.

Dr Michaels insisted that I continue to gargle with salt water, even after I had long since recovered from the bronchitis. He didn't seem too concerned about my voice, but he did suggest that I might have some kind of damage to my vocal cords, and he arranged for me to see an ear, nose & throat specialist in Wollongong. And so it went from there. In their defence, Dr Michaels and all the other doctors I ended up seeing were genuinely baffled. And yes, my situation wasn't something that you might come across every day. But they *were* doctors, and it's astonishing to me, looking back on it now, that none of them undertook more comprehensive medical tests. In the end it was as if they were just grasping at straws. At one stage they even seemed to think I might have tuberculosis. TB, of all things! They did take a chest x-ray at that point, but apart from a few standard blood tests, that was about it for diagnostics.

Anyway, after a few weeks, Mum and I went to Wollongong for my appointment with the ENT specialist. I can't remember his name, but it started with an 'S'. What I do remember is that we travelled for an hour on the bus, and then waited for over two hours to see him. Two hours that felt like forever.

The ENT clinic had a small waiting room that would have ordinarily held about half a dozen people, but all the chairs were taken when we arrived, and the adults that were waiting there had brought lots of children with them too, and they were all doing what little kids do, making noise and generally running amok. On top of the chaos and the claustrophobia, the heat was stifling. I felt like I was breathing hot water.

With the discomfort and the discord of the waiting room to add to the stress, I felt very nervous. I still didn't know what was happening to me, and it was worrying that Dr Michaels didn't know what was happening either.

"She's not normal," I'd heard someone say about me. Okay, so not being 'normal' can be a good thing, but try telling that to a thirteen-year-old girl. I was terrified. I just wanted to go home and curl up in bed with my radio and forget about everything...

Dr Sylvester, that was his name, the ENT specialist. It's strange that it comes to me now, when I've never remembered his name before. I think I must have tried to erase it from my memory, because as soon as I walked into his surgery and saw his beady eyes weighing me up, I knew I was in trouble. He only paid attention to me when he grabbed my chin and poked an orange stick into my mouth and told me to say ahhhh. I glanced helplessly at Mum. Dr Sylvester peered at me with an irritable expression. "I told you to say 'ahhh', girl," he reiterated. Well, I was trying my best to say 'ahhh' - it's just that there was nothing to be heard. And with that and the heat and the stress and Dr Sylvester's impatience, I felt completely overwhelmed. Meanwhile, Dr Sylvester turned back to Mum. "Look at her palms," he said, grabbing my hands. "They're sweaty and she's shaking too. That's not normal." That word again. 'Normal'.

Dr Sylvester said my symptoms were of a "hysterical nature". Then he told me what they did to people who had hysterical symptoms - they had to go to special hospitals where certain procedures were carried out on them "to put their brain right". I shrunk from his words. My insides shrivelled. He was proposing that I should be locked away with all manner of psychos, nuts, and unbalanced people. He was saying I was crazy. I felt panicked and I wanted to throw up. I was sure I wasn't mad - I was just mute. Surely doctors know the difference between mute and mad?

By this time Mum was getting upset as well so Dr Sylvester sent for a nurse to take me into an adjoining room while he continued talking with her. I was distraught. Why couldn't I stay with my mum? I could hear her crying and it sounded like Dr Sylvester was arguing with her. I listened at the door and heard Mum trying to answer back, but her words kept getting stuck between her sobs.

On the long bus ride back home, a sad stress-filled silence settled over us. Looking back on it I can sense something of Mum's internal struggle. She didn't want to believe the doctor, but what if he was right? What if there *was* a cure for me in the 'special hospital'? A week or two in a psychiatric ward, some treatment – no shame in that if it fixed things, if it helped bring my voice back. Right?

My mother might have been in two minds but there was no doubt in my head that being locked away would be a fate worse than death. I was terrified. After the visit to Dr Sylvester I vowed not to see any more doctors. I was literally too scared. At the time I couldn't fully understand everything, but one thing I knew was that I wasn't hysterical - I didn't cry and carry on like hysterical characters did in the movies. So my logic was simple - I thought if I stayed away from the medical fraternity then they wouldn't be able to put me in one of those hospitals. I wasn't going to give anyone the chance to do that to me, even if it meant accepting the loss of my voice.

Back at home Mum started crying again. She seemed to do that a lot in those days. "It'll be alright," she said. "We'll have something nice for dinner, and everything will be fine, and one day, you'll see, one day you'll talk again."

That comment would come back to haunt me throughout the rest of my childhood. "One day her voice will come back," Mum told everyone, almost as if she could bring it about simply by wishing it on me. I know she meant well but it didn't always help. People would get confused. "What is she talking about?" I could see them thinking. "The girl isn't normal."

One morning I couldn't stand it anymore. I decided to run away, back to England. Not knowing where to start, I spent most of the day down at the harbour, hiding in the bushes that used to grow there. I crawled into a space where I could hide but it got cold as night fell so I made my way to the caravan in the backyard of our neighbours' house. It sounds funny, running away to the neighbours, but I didn't find it funny at the time, and neither did Mum and Dad. Beside themselves with worry, they called the police, and the next morning, feeling hungry and defeated, I came home to a lecture from the local sergeant. I nodded glumly as he harangued me.

"Do you know what could have happened to a young girl like you, out by yourself all day and night like that?" I didn't really know - at that age how could I have known? But I nodded again as the policeman gave up with a stern "Don't do it again!"

Having failed in my attempt to run away, I retreated within myself. Being into music, and suddenly not being able to sing, I found myself listening to the radio more than ever. I suppose I built something of a fantasy life around the songs that I loved, putting my own interpretations on them to help me cope with things. Not being able to escape in real life, I looked for escape elsewhere. More and more I would lose myself in daydreams - daydreams where I could speak again, where I was accepted and loved and everything was as it should be. In these dreams I was just like everyone else, and because I had my voice, life went smoothly. I wasn't ignored or left behind like I was in the real world.

I might have been too self-absorbed to appreciate it at the time, but I know that explaining things to our friends and neighbours must have been hard on my parents. We hadn't been given any scientific explanation for my infliction, just a lot of conjecture and innuendo. One doctor did wonder whether a 'viral' infection had somehow attacked my vocal cords and paralysed them, but that theory didn't gain any momentum, and Dr Sylvester had disregarded it.

"Bloody mindedness is what it is," Dad's mate advised him. "I'd give her a good spanking if she was mine." Dad didn't, but I suspect he sometimes wondered if he should. The general public, meanwhile, seemed to think I was deaf, as nine times out of ten people raised their voices a few notches when they talked to me, simplifying their language as though I had lost my marbles and my hearing, as well as my voice. Experiences like these did nothing to increase my self-esteem, and as a result I began to avoid human interaction wherever I could. My lifeline became rock and roll. I spent my waking hours listening to the radio and playing records and I took to going to bed as early as possible so that I could find some respite in sleep.

Over time, Mum got used to the idea of me being mute. She learned to lip-read pretty well, but Dad never mastered it and he would get embarrassed when I wrote notes, especially if we were out somewhere. He didn't mean to be awkward; he just didn't know how to relate to me. My sister Denise thought it was all hilarious. Until the day she got laryngitis herself, that is. Then she immediately panicked, and went screaming to Mum for help, thinking she had gone the same way as me. "Mum, Mum I can't talk anymore, I'm going the same as Marie... Muuuuummmmmm!" Even with the laryngitis her voice still bounced off the walls. Now, h*ere* is someone who's hysterical, I thought. I wondered if we should send her to see Dr Sylvester. What are younger sisters for anyway, except to annoy their older siblings?

CHAPTER 4

*'A bit of a laugh!' That's what my friends thought when I returned
to school without my voice. They suspected it was all a prank. But
they changed their tune over time, when they realised that nothing
they could do or say could make me speak, no matter how much I
wanted to...*

Communicating with someone when you can't talk is a tedious process.
Miming only got me so far, and I was never very good at games of
charades in the first place. Can you imagine having to play charades every
moment of your waking life? The novelty wears off very quickly, I can tell
you. But what else is there? Lip reading isn't easy and since none of us knew
any sign language, it was decided that I should always have a pen and paper
on me to write notes. Written words became my mainstay. Eventually I did
create a sort of sign 'shorthand' for everyday actions such as drinking and
eating, but aside from these and a few other well known gestures (such as the
third finger of the right hand) there was no option but to write everything
down. The trouble was that although writing allowed me to express myself
clearly it was also painfully, painfully s l o w – especially when trying
to share a joke.

Most of the nuns were quite off-handed with me when I came back to
class - I guess they just didn't know what to make of my dilemma. It was okay
while I still had laryngitis, but this ongoing mutism was unprecedented -
none of them had experienced anything like it before. Their response was
pragmatic. "If you can listen, you can learn," I was told. But something of

the joy of learning goes when you can't speak, can't respond, can't interact. I started to withdraw further into myself. It became easier to exist, but not participate; to accept, but to not really try.

My friends in the Elvis group were around, but with the other students and the teachers at St Anne's I found it harder and harder, until eventually I only communicated when I absolutely had to. One or two of the sisters persevered and were helpful but overall I felt that I was being closed out by Father Moran and his kind. "Treat her the same as everyone else," Sister St Patrick decreed with a withering look. "She'll speak when she gets sick of it." Hah! If only it was that easy.

Music was what kept me sane in those days and for all the years ahead, giving me release from my limp and restricted life. I was soothed by song in my bedroom and in the lonely hours in and out of school. Sleep and music became my escapes from my silence, my oppressive world.

Well, it was one thing being into music, but it was another thing altogether to be forced to join the St Anne's choir. A mute in a choir? What a joke. I mean I couldn't even laugh out loud, let alone form any words. I tried to object but the nuns were serious as hell about it. "You're not getting out of this," Sister Theresa insisted. "Just make the shapes with your mouth." Tone deaf, mute or nightingale, it made no difference to her - no one was exempt. Everyone in my class had to be in the school choir for the annual Eisteddfod, including me. As much as I would have loved to be in a choir if I had a voice, I felt beyond foolish just standing there, moving my lips soundlessly.

Eventually, years later, I realised that Sister Theresa had in fact done me a good turn by making me mime. It was one way I could immerse myself further in music, and keep my muscles moving for that time when I hoped and prayed I would speak and sing again. Back then, however, it was beyond embarrassing.

During this time I continued to travel to school each day on the bus. Two buses, actually - I'd get the 7am service from Shellharbour and then switch at Warrawong to get the connecting bus to Dapto. A handful of us St Anne's girls did this trip, but it made for a long day. It was often 5pm before I got home. Then there was dinner and homework and then I was up again at 6am each morning, so I didn't stay up late. Weekends were a reprieve, but apart from Marusia the Elvis girls all lived some distance away, so we didn't see much of each other outside of school.

Marusia lived in Warilla. Her family had emigrated from Scotland so we were sort of kindred spirits as she wasn't accepted as a 'true blue' Aussie either. We had each been called 'pommie bastards' several times. I knew what a bastard was, but I could never understand why I was being called that when my parents were married?

It was Marusia's idea that I try whistling. "It might not be singing, but it's better than nothing," she said. She showed me how to purse my lips and blow through them, the way she did. And of course she was quite talented - she was able to whistle melodies at will. But I was hopeless. I tried my best to follow her instructions, but I never mastered the skill - the best I could manage was a disappointing "pppphhh"!

Marusia and I sometimes wagged school together and would buy hot chips from the takeaway shop near the pool. We used to hide in the sand dunes with our chips like real runaways. Both of our mothers worked at the Shellharbour pub, so we used to hang around the pub car park on weekends. We'd sit in Marusia's mum's car and whenever any guys came over to talk to us we would pretend it was Marusia's car and that we were seventeen. We'd turn up the radio to full volume, playing our parts for all they were worth.

It was outside the Shellharbour pub that Marusia and I met Royce and Pem. They were in their twenties, so we thought we were totally grown up and cool, hanging out with them. One night they picked us up near the harbour and we went to Bass Point, myself pillioned on Royce's motorbike, and Marusia in Pem's car. We stayed later than we meant to and when we returned to the pub our fathers were there, waiting. My dad nearly pulled Royce off his bike before chasing him up the road.

Marusia didn't turn up for school the next day. She couldn't sit down properly for ages, but I got away with it. When Dad took me home I wrote a statement saying we had done nothing (which was true, apart from a bit of innocent kissing and cuddling) and pretending that I thought the boys were only 16. Maybe Dad was lenient because of my situation, but whatever the reason I was lucky - he didn't ask too many questions. He was still disappointed with me but he let me off as long as I promised not to do anything like it again and as long as I didn't tell Mum. I guess he didn't want to upset her.

In the end Marusia and I spent most Saturdays and Sundays that summer at the beach and we both got badly sunburned. In those days cancer awareness wasn't what it is today and neither of us bothered with sunscreen. Mum made up a concoction of olive oil and vinegar in a spray bottle and doused us both in this French dressing. I felt like a walking salad but it worked - the vinegar took away the sting of the sunburn and the oil soothed the skin. After that we walked around in our swimmers wrapped in huge beach towels. We would investigate up and around the rocks to see if we could find anything of value and then we'd watch the lifesavers doing their thing. Hmmm, I thought, as we checked them out in their red and yellow quartered caps. We were still a bit too young for them, but those feelings were somewhere on the horizon. We just needed to develop a little more.

Meanwhile, we planned our weddings and our lives beyond - we decided we would live near each other and that our husbands (David and Donny) would be best mates. We practiced kissing on our arms because we didn't know how to 'pash', but we were pretty naive, really; our thoughts never went any further than that. In the evenings we'd go back to my place and listen to records, or watch TV if there were any good shows on.

Then, in March 1974, David Cassidy came to Australia. David Cassidy! Love of my fourteen year old life! Everyone in the Elvis group went wild when we heard about the tour. Even Mary-Kay, who wasn't a fan, got swept up in the excitement. Plots ran thick as we schemed. The first thing was to get tickets to the concert, of course. That was a must. Then, it was decided, one of us would find out where he was staying and we would all somehow get into his room.

How were we going to pull off this plan? Well, Darlene came up with an ingenious idea: we would mail ourselves to him. In a box. Yep, that could work, we thought. It sounded good. Anything to get in there. But what we were going to do after we got into his room? Umm... Well, you can't plan everything, can you. Some things you just have to leave to fate - everyone knows that.

It was one of the hottest days that summer when Mum and Dad drove us up to Randwick Racecourse in Sydney. There was a long queue but eventually we handed over our tickets and ran forward with our hormones running high. The stage was MASSIVE and flanked with huge speakers. I had never been to a pop concert before so all this was a new experience, but it was everything that I had dreamed of. And it was LOUD. The music was so loud you couldn't hear anyone speak. I thought it was just the right place for me.

We took up position near the front of the stage and held our ground but nothing had prepared us for the madness when the concert started and David came on stage, wearing flared white dungarees. Neil Diamond's 'Crunchy Granola Suite' was playing as he entered and all of a sudden we were separated, pulled apart by the surge of the crowd. I was crushed against the security barrier. Something hit me in the head.

After several hours of waiting in line in the summer heat, and with all the excitement and the knock on the head, darkness came rushing over me like an unstoppable wave. I had to be pulled out of the mass of bodies and taken to the first aid tent for water and a rest. Aaaarrgghhhh! I wished I could have screamed out loud! All that anticipation, and now here I was, lying down with an ice pack on the back of my head. I wasn't the only one, either - it turned out that a part of the stage had collapsed in the melee and several girls had been injured. They even had to stop the performance for a few minutes while they made repairs. I could still hear David when he started up again with 'Daydreamer', but I couldn't see anything. I had to wait until it came on TV before I saw the whole show.

In case you're wondering, we didn't end up crashing David's hotel room in a box. We gave up on that idea when we saw his bodyguards. They were big and they looked mean. And there were hundreds of girls already there at the hotel by the time we arrived, probably planning the same thing as us - it was all just a bit overwhelming.

"Hmmmm," Mary-Kay said, as we walked away. "Elvis wouldn't have been like that. He's a gentleman; we would have got to meet him." I had to smile. 'Of course we would, Mary-Kay, 'cause you just know Elvis personally, don't you?' I thought. 'He would have pointed to us in the crowd as he shook his hips, wouldn't he? "Bring them girls there," he would have said in that deep sultry voice of his...' I might have been silent but as I imagined this scenario my whole body started shaking with laughter. I had to hold on to my knees to avoid falling over. We must have all been thinking the same thing, because one by one the other girls all joined in, giving voice to my mirth.

The girls in the Elvis group helped bolster my spirits but throughout this time my school life was slowly disintegrating. And as I was getting into more and more trouble I never told Mum what was really happening. I don't know why. Maybe it goes back to Nana and her advice, or maybe it was fear of the old presumption that if you were punished at school then you must have done something wrong.

Of course it would have been much better to explain things to Mum, but instead of opening up to her, I started ignoring her. It was almost as if I was taking my pain and frustration out on her by refusing to let her in. I guess I just didn't believe she could understand what I was going through, and because of this I was stubborn and surly at every turn. I read somewhere that teenagers are all like that during puberty, and that they get over it eventually, but there were also other manifestations of the stress that I was experiencing. I wasn't eating properly, and I had recurrent stomach aches and headaches. I was pretty sure that these symptoms had nothing to do with puberty.

One morning I left the house to catch the bus and I turned around for some reason. I could see Mum in the window, watching me walk away - she had her hand over her mouth as if she was stifling a sob. I had been mean to her again. I had thrown my breakfast in the bin, and also the lunch she made me. I had given her 'evil looks' for no real reason, other than I was upset and taking my stresses out on her. In that moment, when I saw her through the window, I got a glimpse of how it was affecting her. I wanted to cry. I wanted to go back home and tell her I didn't want to be mean to her or to anyone else, it was just that I was unhappy at St Anne's. I wanted to hug her and tell her I loved her...

But I didn't go back. I turned away and walked on, in time for the bus to the living hell that school had become.

CHAPTER 5

The downward slope of my life steepened dramatically when Father Moran started accusing me of being in league with the Devil. It's easy to wonder how different things might have been if only I could've faced him down, but the idea of facing down a priest is not something that occurs to a frightened and impressionable Catholic girl...

In the 1970s the parish priest was still effectively the head of the local Catholic school. Our principal, Sister Gerard, was nominally in charge at St Anne's, but she and the other nuns that taught us all looked to Father Moran as their leader. So when Father Moran took an increasingly negative attitude towards me, he set an example for my teachers to follow.

Within a few weeks of losing my voice Father Moran and Sisters Kathryn and St Patrick reasoned that as the doctors couldn't find anything physically wrong with me then God must be punishing me for something that I had done. They concluded that I needed to confess my sins to receive God's forgiveness. I thought the idea was ridiculous but Sister St Patrick insisted. "You're not getting out of Confession on Thursdays," she said. "You can write down what you want to confess."

Every Thursday the whole school would go to confession, in readiness for Mass. We wore maroon berets with our school uniforms, because girls wore hats to church in those days. All the students would wait in line down the side of St John's, waiting for their turn to enter the church and confess their sins. I wasn't the only one trying to think of something to confess. While the Elvis group were waiting in line we would sometimes 'swap sins'.

Mary-Kay made an art of it. "I forgot my night time prayers again last night," she might say, "so you take that one this week, Cassandra, and I'll take your swearing at your mum."

As the line inched forward into the church the smell of dust and incense was overpowering. I'd pray to be able to confess to Father Carr, but it always seemed to be Father Moran in the confessional box. By the time I was next in line I'd be sweating and feeling nauseous. I had already written out my little piece of paper and when Father Moran opened the grille, I'd slip my note through to him.

Father Moran usually read the note and told me to say six Hail Mary's and several Our Fathers, and I always left feeling a lot 'dirtier' than when I went in. Funny, because confession is supposed to make you feel clean and reborn. A weight is supposed to be lifted from your shoulders, not added to them.

Well, this particular week I had pinched a few coins from Dad's wallet to buy sweets for me and Denise, and I'd been feeling terrible about it. Maybe I should have swapped with Mary- Kay, but I decided to do the right thing - I asked God to forgive me and I promised not to do it again. When I reached the confessional box Father Moran snatched the note from me. "Hrumph," he grunted. I wasn't sure if it was a blessing or not but he didn't say anything else, so I left as quickly as I could.

Anonymity was already denied me by having to write my confessions, but I only truly learned how much my privacy had been betrayed when I was called up to the principal's office later that day. My confessional note was there in Sister Gerard's hand, and now I had to answer to her, as well as to God, for my sins. Taking a bit of money from Dad's pocket didn't seem like a major crime to me, but I was treated as if I'd robbed a bank. Several banks. With a gun! A stormy looking Father Moran stood behind Sister Gerard with his arms folded across his chest. He had told Sister Gerard to call me in, to 'discuss' my attitude surrounding my faith, or lack thereof.

My confession hadn't been good enough for Father Moran. He was sure I hadn't told him everything, that I had more to confess. "Why are you slapping God in the face like this? Why are you so stubborn?" he asked. "You have no right to betray the Church this way."

I tried to write a note for Sister Gerard but Father Moran snatched it away and tore it up. He was convinced that I was trying to trick her. He went on to say that if I did not come clean and tell God everything, he would have no choice but to keep me apart from the other girls so that I couldn't corrupt them. If I refused to confess my sins honestly then I couldn't take communion and therefore it was no use going to mass at all.

Well, I might not have been able to say anything but my heart was pounding. I just had to get out of there. When Sister Gerard dismissed me I ran outside and around the back of St John's Church where I slithered down the wall and cried. I thought of Nana as I cried. I felt that God had turned against me.

Father Moran didn't even read the note I wrote Sister Gerard that day in her office, asking why they had discussed my confidential confession. I asked that they please stop telling me how bad I was, because I wasn't doing anything wrong. I was just coming to school and keeping my head down, I tried to explain. Then I was going home and crawling into bed so I could ignore the rest of the world.

Things were bad enough already, but they only got worse from there. Sister St Patrick in particular started pulling me up at every opportunity. She constantly chastised me about my behaviour and my 'ungodly' attitude. God had taken my voice as a punishment for my sins, she said, and she made me stand outside religious instruction classes until such time as I came to my senses and realised that I was possessed by the devil. Hellfire and brimstone were promised for my just desserts if I wouldn't reform.

Maybe one teacher saying these things wouldn't have mattered so much, but Sister St Patrick was backed up by Sister Kathryn and Father Moran and the full weight of the Catholic institution. I lost count of the number of times Father Moran told me I was a woman of the devil in the coming months. I thought it was quite ironic at first because I didn't think I was much of a woman yet, but after a while all the negative attention was like water torture. Drip, drip, drip, drip, gradually breaking me down, dripping, dripping, steadily, constantly. The accusations and innuendos began to erode my already fragile self-confidence. I began to doubt myself. Was I actually bad, like they believed? I began to question everything I thought I knew.

Terence Griffin was my cousin on Mum's side of the family, but we'd practically lived together as one big family back in Bolton before he joined the army. He was ten years older than me and I thought of him as the big brother I always wanted. He was tall, handsome and happy-go-lucky. I adored Terry and had spent most of my early Christmases together with him and his three sisters.

Terry was a bombardier in the British army's 88 Arracan Battery Royal Artillery. Ever since we'd moved to Australia Terry had been looking into the process of being seconded so he could join us, but at that time the 'Troubles' in Northern Ireland were escalating out of control. Peace talks had broken down amidst a cycle of increasing violence and the British government had imposed direct rule in Belfast. Terry and I often wrote to each other, and he always joked that if he got caught by the IRA he would tell them he was an Aussie to confuse them.

Then one afternoon I got the biggest surprise - there was Terry, just outside my bedroom window, standing on our front door step, about to knock on the door. In my silent voice I cried out in happiness. "Oh my God, Terry? Terry, is it really you?" Terence turned and smiled when he saw me. He put his hand flat against the window pane, and I placed mine to his, like we always used to when we were children.

I was beyond happy to see Terry. Finally I had someone in my life who would help me. I knew he would knock them sideways when I told him everything that was happening at school. I was ecstatic. For just a moment everything was going to be ok.

But then he was somewhere else.

I feel uneasy, I'm not sure why.
I hear voices. Happy voices.
Laughing voices. Then I hear screaming.
I feel pain.
Excruciating pain.
In my back.
In my stomach.
    Unbearable searing pain cutting through me.
And horror.
Unbelievable horror.
Rising through me, Suffocating me.

It felt like I'd been punched in the back by something huge and heavy and forceful. I saw blue and white lights all around me, and when the shock receded I was left nauseous and dizzy. I could hear something but I wasn't sure what it was. Then everything went black.

Eventually I stir, aware again.
Terry is there, but he isn't there.
I know inside me that he is dead.

I don't know how long I was unconscious. When I came around, I was at the back of St John's church where I sometimes hid. I didn't know what I was doing there and I felt confused, but gradually things came back to me. I'd had another bad day at school. I wasn't feeling well and I needed to go somewhere quiet. Classes had just finished and I had sneaked into the church to be by myself.

I remembered closing my eyes and listening to the background noises: girls chattering and laughing, car doors slamming. I heard the school buses come and go but I didn't want to move, I just wanted to stay there in peace, feeling removed from everything. I must have fallen asleep, but it wasn't a dream, I knew it wasn't. It was too real. Terry's smile, his hand on the window. The pain. Something was wrong. 'Oh God,' I thought, 'what's happening? Why are you doing this to me?'

I run out of the church, pain still racking my stomach and back, and crashed straight into Sister Eloise. Sister Eloise was the only one of the nuns I trusted at the time. My tears messed up the words as I scribbled down my vision but she did her best to reassure me. "It's only a nightmare," she said. "You must be very tired to fall asleep in the church, it's so uncomfortable in there." *But what about Terry?* I underlined several times. I was still very upset and scared. I knew something wasn't right but Sister Eloise was more worried about how I was going to get home as I had missed the last school bus. She decided to ask Father Carr for help.

Father Carr was always patient with me. Whenever I complained about school his advice was to just keep my head down and wait - I would soon be sixteen and be able to leave. Then I'd be free to live life as I wanted. Father Carr was just out of the seminary and only a few years older than us himself, so I felt I could relate to him. He genuinely cared about all the girls at St Anne's and he always gave me a little smile or a nod of the head when our paths crossed.

When Sister Eloise brought me to him that afternoon, Father Carr sincerely tried to comfort me. I knew he was being kind but I still couldn't shake the awful feeling that something was terribly wrong. After a while he offered to drive me home in his VW Beetle. In any other circumstances I would have been pleased as punch but that afternoon I just stared out the window as we drove. My silence felt more oppressive than ever. When we got to Shellharbour Father Carr told my parents that I had been "feeling unwell" at school and suggested that I stay home for a few days. Mum made him a cup of tea and he stayed chatting for a while. Nothing specific was said about my vision of Terry. It was almost as if it hadn't happened at all. After Father Carr left I went to bed, but I could still hear my parents talking in the kitchen. I heard Dad tell Mum it wasn't right that I slept so much.

Mum came in to check on me later that night, but when I shared my vision with her she said the same as the others. "Don't be silly Marie, you must have fallen asleep and just didn't realise it." After a few days, however, she was getting concerned herself - I still hadn't gotten out of bed or eaten anything. I felt morose and I couldn't escape the feeling that something terrible had happened to Terry. Mum wanted to take me to the doctor but I didn't want to go.

I hated doctors by this stage. I just wanted everyone to leave me alone.

When I finally returned to school again I wasn't allowed to communicate with my friends anymore, just as Father Moran had threatened. I still saw them of course, but we could only sneak notes to each other when the nuns weren't looking. At lunch times I had to sit by myself on the bench outside the classroom so the sisters could keep an eye on me. I couldn't explain how I felt and it wouldn't have done any good even if I could. My fate at St Anne's was sealed. "You're a woman of the devil," spat Father Moran, for the upteenth time. "You're not to come into my church until you repent." Every Friday from then on I was to stand outside the church while the rest of the school attended Mass.

I wondered if there was anything other than my loss of voice that made Father Moran associate me with the devil. Had Sister Eloise told him about my vision? Was there a mark on my forehead or a look in my eyes only identifiable by a priest? Was it something to do with my curly hair, or the way I walked? I didn't feel like a bad person, and I knew for a fact that some of the blonde haired, blue eyed 'angelic' girls at St Anne's didn't even need to make up their confessions like the rest of us did. As school life became more miserable the prospect of expulsion crossed my mind, but even that hope was dashed. "Because of my Christian charity," Father Moran declared, "I will allow you to stay on at this school."

The stone walls of the church were uncomfortable to lean against - they were slimy in the rain and sharp in all weather. Banished from the Mass, I indulged in any fantasy that would make my life more bearable as I waited outside. I visited Nana in England, and I went to America to meet Kurt Russell. I sang Elvis songs in my head - but not 'In the Ghetto' because Sister Kathryn said it was about abortion and we weren't allowed to think about that.

Around this time Mum gave me her prayer book, in the hope that it would help me. The cover was made of mother of pearl and the book had been a present from her sister Mary when she was fourteen, but when Sister St Patrick found me with it I got the cane. The prayer book was written in Latin, and the Catholic Church in Australia had outlawed Latin Mass in 1969, so Sister Gerard took it away and hid it in her desk. I couldn't believe it. The next Friday while they were at Mass I went to her office and took it back but then, when she found out, I got the cane yet again. As far as the school was concerned I could now add 'thief' to my list of transgressions.

Throughout all this I was slowly being shut out of the social interactions that are so vital to teenagers. Even my connection with the Elvis group was viewed with suspicion by the nuns, and not wanting my friends to get into trouble I stayed away, withdrawing further and further into myself. Any pleasant or understanding voices, looks or actions that came my way were swamped by distrust and accusations. I felt like a beetle in a glass jar, shaken and stared at, prodded and poked, cut off from any chance of freedom. If I wasn't ignored I was watched, whispered about and picked on. All in all I was trapped, unable to escape the malice that disturbed my days and haunted me every night.

CHAPTER 6

Drugs. I read recently that something like 70% of all Americans take one prescription or another. I don't know how that compares with Australia, but I know that Louise's little white pills helped me escape the crushing reality that I found myself facing every day as a young teenage girl. I know more about these things now but I didn't think about the legality or the consequences at the time - I just wanted to be able to survive the torture that life at school had become.

Despite everything I tried to get on with my classes. I wanted to learn, I really did. It wasn't that I was ever a bad student, it was just that circumstances were conspiring against me. It's difficult to focus on studying when you're constantly being chastised. Father Moran had decreed that I was trouble, so most days trouble is what I found, even when I was on my best behaviour. I was still doing okay in English and science, but the other subjects... well, what can I say; they were taught by Sister Kathryn and her kind.

As I was clearly miserable my friend Louise suggested that I take some 'happy' pills that her mother had 'given' her. She said they were really helpful when you weren't feeling well and didn't want to go to school. So I started taking the little white pills with her each morning when we boarded the bus at Warrawong. At first they weren't too bad - they made me feel funny. Not funny as in strange, I mean funny as in happy. With the help of the little white pills I found I could silently giggle at what the sisters were saying, and even think up a few comebacks if they were mean. Of course I never actually expressed these comebacks - the thoughts just stayed in my head - but for a while the pills did actually help me cope. They took the edge off.

But then strange things started to happen. One time I fell off my chair in class, but when I stood up I realised I hadn't fallen off the chair at all. Then I went to get on the bus after school and missed the door. I walked right into the side of the bus. I was odd enough already, being the voiceless girl, but now I was behaving erratically as well. I guess I was making a spectacle of myself but to be honest, I hardly felt as if I was there. It didn't even hurt when I got the cane or was hit by Father Moran's famous tennis racquet anymore - there was a tingle, but then I found the whole thing very funny.

When the effect of the pills wore off I would feel sleepy. But I was sleeping a lot those days already, so it didn't strike Mum or Dad as particularly strange if I went to bed early. There didn't seem to be any other side effects, but I was naturally frugal anyway. Most days Louise would give me a couple of pills but sometimes I kept them or only took one. It depended on how bad I felt that morning; how much help I felt I needed to get me through the day. The rest of the pills I saved up, just in case. You never know what the future will hold.

In the meantime I still saw the Elvis group girls when I could. The nuns were doing their best to keep us separated at school and apart from Marusia we didn't live near each other, but sometimes they would come over to my place or Mum would drop me off at one of their houses on the weekends. I lived for these interactions. Social life is everything to a teenage girl, and it was all the more so for me as I became increasingly ostracised at school.

I particularly liked spending days at Courtney's house. Her mum would make these tiny little donuts for us and we would scoff them down before her brother realised they were there for the taking. Then we would walk around the streets of Dapto on a sugar high, and I would listen to Courtney talking about what we'd do when we left school. That was her favourite subject. That and boys. And more boys.

Around this time Mum found an advertisement in the Mercury for the Illawarra Girls Choir. I might have been voiceless but my sister Denise had always liked singing too, so the three of us started catching the bus to town once a week so that she could join the choir practice at the Wollongong Baptist Church. Mum and I would sit at the back of the hall and listen as they belted out 'Carol of the Birds' and 'The Three Drovers' and other songs. The choir leader had a thing for Australiana and at Christmas and other special occasions the girls would all dress up in their long green dresses with the fashionable bell sleeves and go performing. I remember Mum and I accompanying them to Bowral for the Tulip festival, where they sang 'Tulips in Amsterdam', with a few changes. "When it's spring again, we'll see again tulips in Bowral town," they sang. It was quirky but the locals loved it.

On one occasion the pastor of the church came over and introduced himself after choir practice. He was friendly and well-meaning, but my experiences with Father Moran had made me mistrustful of men of the cloth. When the pastor eventually asked Mum what had happened to me she gave him the standard spiel, ending with her usual "oh, but she will get her voice back one day." I cringed but the pastor looked me in the eyes and told me he was sure that Mum was right. He then leaned towards me and whispered that he would pray for me, even if I didn't want him to. Hmmm, I thought; were the thoughts in my mind really that obvious?

Because Sister St Patrick was the school counsellor at St Anne's, we were supposed to go to her if we had any problems. It was her job to look after the 'emotional well being' of the girls at school but the truth was that she looked after some girls a lot more than others. Even without taking my 'eccentricity' into account, the girls in the Elvis group were already outsiders. Our fathers all worked in the steel works and Marusia and I were recent immigrants to boot. That shouldn't have made any difference, but it did. Sister St Patrick didn't seem to want to help us the way she helped some of the other girls. I remember her telling us we weren't allowed to have tennis lessons on sports day, for example. "Your parents don't have the money to pay for it," she said, as though that explained everything.

It was all too clear by this point that Sister St Patrick really didn't like me. Of course there were other girls she didn't like as well, but for some reason she always seemed to aim the brunt of her malice at me. One day I was in the library, one of the few places I felt at ease, and suddenly there she was, barrelling towards me. She must have had a bad day, or reached her threshold or whatever. "I'm sick of you, wretched girl, grabbing all the attention," she hissed. "It's time you stopped all this nonsense."

I suppose Sister St Patrick genuinely believed that I was making it all up, and that I could talk if I simply chose to, but for the benefit of her conscience she had arranged for me to see a psychiatrist at St Vincent's Hospital in Sydney. She wrote Mum a letter, informing her of the appointment. Apparently my whole family had to go along for the interview.

As I was leaving the library that day Sister St Patrick tore strips off me again, just for good measure. "Don't you know the trouble you are causing?" she muttered. My dream about Terence had obviously been disturbing her. "Mrs Oberon has recently lost her mother, whom she loved her very much," she said. "Now, why would your cousin appear to you, and her mother not appear to her?" I didn't know anything about this Mrs Oberon or her mother, but how could I answer that question, even if I did know them? It wasn't like I had planned to have that vision of Terry. And it's not like there had been any benefit to me. Terry was my favourite cousin and I was traumatised by what I had 'seen'. I didn't know how to respond as Sister St Patrick stared at me, her eyes bulging, waiting for an impossible answer from a frightened and voiceless girl. I shrugged my shoulders; I was genuinely at a loss. "You have to stop lying," Sister St Patrick spat, turning on her heels with a dismissive wave of her hand.

Two weeks later Mum and Dad and Denise and I took the two-hour drive up to St Vincent's in Sydney to see the psychiatrist. Denise was quite miffed at having to come along. I remember her whining to Mum: 'Why do I have to go? I'm not batty, *Marie* is!" I glared at Denise but she made a point of looking the other way. Mum said it was all nonsense, but if the school thought it was for the best, then who was she to argue? From her point of view the sisters were only trying to help. "One day we'll all have a good laugh about this," she said, turning to me with a forced smile.

The psychiatrist was a short fat man who looked at me over the top of his glasses and never once changed his expression. He was neither welcoming nor condemning, but I had no reason to trust him. After all, I hadn't had a good run with doctors so far. At first he questioned me alone, barraging me with questions. I can't clearly remember the details but I think I mostly just nodded. What I do remember clearly is feeling panicked when it occurred to me that he might keep me there at St Vincent's. I was terrified. After a while he brought the rest of the family into the consulting room. At one point he suggested that my parents might have mistreated me, at which point Dad stormed out. "I don't have to listen to this," he shouted.

The psychiatrist was just doing his job, but I don't think he understood what it was actually like for me or for my parents. He wasn't alone there - no one really understood. How could they, unless they had experienced the same thing themselves? I had already been labelled 'a psychological case' by Dr Michaels, and in a small town like Shellharbour, doctor-patient confidentiality wasn't always that confidential. Some of the neighbours wouldn't let me be around their children because I was thought to be 'mad'. I was told by one of my parents' friends that they wouldn't talk to me if I wouldn't talk to them. It became clear to me that very few people actually *wanted* to understand. Another 'friend' of the family said people like me should be locked away for the safety of the community. I was standing right there when she gave her opinion to Mum. "Be careful," she said. "If her mind is going then you never know what might happen next."

I experienced it all. The jibes, the finger pointing, the whispering, the stares when I walked down the street. But I couldn't answer back; I couldn't say anything to defend myself or dissuade those that judged me. Looking back on it, they had already made up their minds anyway. Many of them wouldn't even let me write an explanation down on paper. They wouldn't give me the time. Even now I find it hard to put into words exactly how it made me feel... Imagine feeling totally isolated. Imagine being made to feel like a freak, unfit to be around 'normal' people. Slowly but surely an unanswerable anger was setting in. It didn't necessarily show, but a seething resentment was building up, deep inside me.

In later years I often wondered how differently I might have been treated if I had lost my voice to an 'identifiable' cause. How much help would I have received if I had lost my voice due to cancer, for example? Would the community around me at school and at home have felt more sympathy then, rather than ostracising me? Was the way they treated me simply a reflection of their unknowing? Their fear of the unknown? Is it really so easy to condemn someone as a liar or a devil-worshipper, just because there is an absence of a medical explanation for their condition? Do we still live in witch-hunting times?

Despite my anger and my fear, the session with the psychiatrist ended up being a rare moment of affirmation, because at the conclusion of the interview he told my parents that he considered me to be a perfectly normal teenager. He said that he didn't think there was anything psychologically wrong with me - I was just a fourteen year old girl going through the difficulties of puberty with the added stress of having lost my voice. He suggested that they should just let me do what teenage girls do: go to school, meet up with friends, the usual stuff. He wrote it all up in a report and sent a copy to St Anne's.

Sister St Patrick freaked out when she read the report, of course - this wasn't what she wanted to hear. She called me a liar again, and said that if the psychiatrist considered me normal then I must have bewitched him. She dragged me off to see Sister Gerard, and demanded I be sent for another assessment because I shouldn't be allowed to get away with it. She said that she had a duty to protect *all* the girls at St Anne's and she implied that I was in some way a threat to my classmates and peers. Sister Gerard took a deep breath. I think she'd had enough already. She waited for Sister St Patrick to vent her spleen. Then she sighed and told me to go back to class.

CHAPTER 7

The psychiatrist might have decided that I was perfectly normal, but that wasn't good enough for Sister St Patrick or Father Moran, who continued to single me out. I tried to be pragmatic, to stay out of trouble, but it didn't make any difference. It wasn't long before trouble found me again, and when it did, it was worse than ever.

As the school term rolled on we studied the subject of war and peace in English class. Each of us had to present an assignment, so I focussed on the problems between England and Ireland. I decided to make it personal and include Terry - this would be a good way of exorcising my vision, I thought. Pushing my fears to the back of my mind, I wrote to Terry. I told him that I'd dreamed of him but I didn't dare mention the details. I asked him to write back to me as soon as he could.

Terry hadn't written back to me by the day the assignment was due. I told myself he was fine, everything was okay, but my pulse raced whenever I thought of him. I remember those words echoing in my mind when I handed my project in to Ms Widdows. "He's fine. Everything is okay." It was like the words had sharp edges - as though they were cutting me up inside. My heart tightened. I felt sick.

I had lots of paper clippings about the skirmishes with the IRA that Mum had brought with her from England. I also had my own experience of Ireland to draw on - when I was a child we had been on holiday in Belfast when we were woken up in the night and told we had to leave, because of the bombings. I remembered how dazed and tired we were, and how our suitcases bulged from being packed so hurriedly.

It was cold while we waited for the ferry to take us back to England. The adults were whispering furtively and looking around as if they were expecting something awful, but us kids thought we were on a daring adventure, being moved in the middle of the night and boarding a ferry to be smuggled back to safety in England. It wasn't until I wrote my assignment that I understood the impact of the bombings and began to appreciate how we had escaped real danger that night.

I grew up with mixed feelings about Ireland. Our family were thought of as traitors to the Irish cause by some, even though we had Irish heritage ourselves and my great grandmother was known to have run a safe house for Fenian Irish republicans. Nana returned to Ireland regularly for holidays and wouldn't let us forget our roots, but Terry was an English soldier and therefore the enemy. It all made for an interesting and highly personal assignment.

I included Terry's picture and Mum's clippings together with my essay into a cardboard folder that I made out of an old shoebox. The cardboard was the same grey as the newsprint, and the newsprint rubbed off on my hands and smudged when I touched it. It made me think of the charcoal grime that coated the factories and the houses back in Bolton. One of the clippings described how Terry's regiment had been shot at by the IRA on several occasions. I wrote in my notes that Terry always seemed to be in the wrong place at the wrong time.

Ms Widdows was a lay teacher, rather than a nun. Unlike Sister Kathryn and her kind, Ms Widdows was the type of teacher who actually made you want to learn, and I loved her. She always found inspiring ways to teach us, and she was into music, just like me and my friends were. When Ms Widdows found me and the Elvis girls listening to my little radio she decided to use the experience in a positive way. I can only imagine that Sister St Patrick or

Sister Kathryn would have confiscated the radio and put us all in detention, but Ms Widdows played us some popular songs in class instead. Looking back on it I'm surprised she got away with it, but I guess the sisters probably didn't know. Anyway, she was my hero at the time. After we listened to the songs we had to pull the lyrics apart and write an essay on their meaning. What an interesting class! One of the songs she played was 'The Sound of Silence' by Simon and Garfunkel. Most of the girls thought that it was about not hearing, about being deaf, but I saw something else in the lyrics, something deeper: it wasn't about not hearing, I wrote; it was more about not speaking up, of staying silent, of welcoming the darkness.

One day our English class went on excursion to the newly opened Sydney Opera House. We saw a performance of 'Dalgerie' by the Australian composer James Penberthy. It was about an Aboriginal girl who'd had an affair with a white man and was waiting for him to return to her. I thought the opera itself was the usual 'love and lost' story, but I was thrilled to be in such a huge, beautiful building, and there were so many things to take in apart from the performance. The Opera House itself is a majestic place, and I was also fascinated by the stage production - the lights and all the other things that go on behind the scenes. Later that night we attended a ballet. We were so lucky, an opera and a ballet in one day. I wonder how Ms Widdows managed to talk Sister Gerard into letting us go.

On the way back home Jo Crocker was at the front of the bus as usual, flirting with the bus driver as she always did. If one of the other girls dobbed her in she would be in trouble again. But then she would bash them. Jo was top dog of St Anne's and she let everyone know it, but she never bothered me or my friends. To us she was just Jo, that's the way she was, her school shirt ripped at the shoulders to emulate her hero Paul Hogan. The cane was a daily routine for Jo but she was funny and bubbly, and nothing ever got her down. She would take her punishment and carry on as if nothing had happened.

Jo got me thinking that day. Maybe I could be more like her, I thought. I had been given a glimmer of hope by Ms Widdows and I wondered if I could build up some resilience to the nuns and Father Moran and get by, despite their condemnations. It seemed to work for Jo. For a brief moment in time I believed that everything could change for the better. And yes, everything was about to change, but not in the way I wanted. Some things just take on a life of their own and sometimes there is nothing you can do to stop them...

It started out like any other school day; the bus came at 7am like it always did. Most of the girls who got on the bus at Shellharbour went to St Mary's College, and thought themselves a better class of person than the St Anne's girls. The rule of the day was that if you didn't make it into St Mary's College you went to St Anne's, but the St Mary's girls didn't seem much different to me. I couldn't join in their conversations, as it would take too long to write everything down, so I just listened. After they got used to me they ignored me most of the time.

When I got to school I found out that Ms Widdows had given me top marks for my war and peace project. She drew me aside after class and gave me a set of pens and a book. She said that she knew I was having a hard time at school, and wished she could help me. She said my project was the best she had ever seen in her class, and she advised me to keep writing and never give up. Her theory was that because I had lost my voice, my ability to write was making up for it.

Ms Widdows and I 'talked' about Terry and I told her about my terrible premonition. It was a slow conversation as I had to write everything down, but she was very patient. We talked about how I felt hounded by Sister St Patrick and by Father Moran. Ms Widdows told me that life would take its course. She told me to keep my head down and to put all other thoughts aside for now. Like Father Carr, she said things would change when I was a little older - when I was sixteen I could always leave school and find my own way in life.

Ms Widdows said that she had no doubt that I would make something of myself. She reassured me that I had no demons in me - I was just confused and a little lost, which she said was usual for teenagers anyway, but more so for me, given my condition. I loved Ms Widdows, and I was content for a few hours glowing in the knowledge that at least one of my teachers thought I was worthwhile, and that I had done a good job on my project.

I floated home that afternoon. I remember the smell of the hot summer. On the bus ride to Warrawong I showed Marusia and Louise the book Ms Widdows had given me. I remember the delicious battered savs that we celebrated with at Warrawong while I waited for the connecting bus home.

And then the world fell apart.

Mum had received a telegram from England that afternoon, confirming my worst fears. As soon as I opened the door and saw Mum crying, Terry's face flashed before me, just as I had seen it in my vision. I saw his hand against mine on the window. I saw the bright lights and I felt again the punch in the back that I felt that day in the church.

They called it the M62 coach bombing, named after the motorway where it happened, between Manchester and Leeds. The bus was full of soldiers and their families. It was after midnight when the blast ripped through the vehicle, and I'm sure Terry must have been sleeping. Maybe he was dreaming that he was visiting me when the back end of the bus was completely blown apart. At the other end of the bus, the driver was lacerated by shards of broken glass as the windows exploded, but he somehow managed to bring the vehicle to a stop, saving the remaining passengers. The newspapers said it was one of the worst IRA bombings in Britain. Nine soldiers were dead, including Terry. The wife of one of the soldiers died as well, together with her children, aged five and two years old.

There was very little left of Terry's body. They said he had been seated right above the bomb when the bus blew up. Parts of him were found more than two hundred metres away. I saw the pictures in the newspaper that were later sent from England. I recognised some of his LP records, scattered around the bomb site. I saw the paisley shirt that he wore on leave. He'd been wearing that shirt in the photo of him that I'd included with my assignment. He looked cool.

I ran outside to the backyard and curled up under the banana tree. I lay there for a long time, struggling to breathe. The cicadas were chirping and I could hear the birds flying overhead but I was in a void. I felt like I had been sucked through some kind of tunnel. I felt nothing but fear and pain.

In my vision, had I seen him before or after he died? Had he been saying goodbye to me?

Was it a warning of what was going to happen? Was it because I loved him, because we were close? Or was it because I was the Devil's woman, like Father Moran claimed? My mind flooded with grief and guilt, uncertainty and loss. I had never really believed the accusations that I was evil, but now I truly began to wonder. I didn't know any more. I just didn't know.

Who can I ask? Who can I tell?

I see flashbacks of my vision.

Terry waves good-bye.

The pain.

I feel again the pain.

He's smiling at me through my bedroom window.

He knocks on the door... There's no one.

I was completely stunned when I eventually came back inside. We didn't have a telephone in the house back then so we had to go to the Police Station for Mum to take a call from Aunt Annie. Annie told Mum the whole story, how Terence had been killed, and the police gave us copies of the newspapers from England. The headlines said that the bus bombing was a terrible tragedy, but I don't remember it ever making the Australian news. Before we went home I was questioned about my 'dream' again, because Mum told the police that I knew it had happened, and that I had been right. The policeman stared at me but Mum did most of the talking. I just nodded my head.

I remember Dad saying "shut up Veronica," as he sometimes did when she went on about things.

I was a mess the next day at school. I was told off, censored and called out for inattention several times. I held out until recess but then I couldn't manage anymore. I broke down. My friend Courtney sat with me while I tried to explain everything to her. Courtney put her arm around me as I wrote paragraph after paragraph of tear-smudged notes. On top of the overwhelming sadness I felt, I was also frustrated by my voicelessness. Not being able to speak made any meaningful communication a huge effort. I showed Courtney the newspaper clippings and the telegram. My whole body ached and I couldn't stop weeping. Courtney was worried for me. She tried to find help, but of course Sister St Patrick was the first person she bumped into.

"How can you make up such a story?" Sister St Patrick bayed, hands flung high in horror. "How can a child be so wicked? You'll burn in the fires of hell for this." Then, despite Courtney's best efforts, she stormed off, refusing to look at the evidence.

It was a hell of a day. I remember trying to concentrate on a science exam that afternoon, but being completely unable to. My tears just kept falling on the paper in front of me. Sister Gerard reprimanded me too - she said I had to get used to death. I might have expected some sympathy from her, or at least some kind of recognition that I hadn't just made up my vision of Terry, but it was not to be.

The only teacher that believed me was Ms Widdows. She was shocked, just like my close friends were. First the vision, then the proof - she said the connection couldn't be denied. Ms Widdows was certain that Terry was saying goodbye to me in my vision. She said she had heard of that kind of thing before and that it wasn't something to be scared of. But I couldn't stop crying, and I didn't know what to do.

Seeing me so distraught, Mary-Kay and some of the other Elvis girls decided we should have a séance to try and contact Terry. It might sound like a crazy idea, but they honestly meant well. They chipped away at my misgivings until I eventually gave in to their arguments. Maybe Terry really did want to tell me something and this would be an opportunity to hear him out. "Jesus won't mind, because Terry's your cousin," Mary-Kay said. "We'll just make sure that he's alright and in heaven. That can't be wrong, can it?"

CHAPTER 8

The séance was really very innocent. We were just girls playing around with something new, and we certainly didn't mean any harm. But that's not the way Father Moran saw it when he caught us with our scrabble set and our amateur Ouija board that day. Looking back on it now, I still don't know if we really made contact with Terry or if there is another explanation for what happened. What I do know is that the way it was dealt with, I was pushed too far. Enough was enough.

The idea of having a séance quickly gathered momentum among my friends. "My mother's a spirit medium," Louise said, crossing her arms. "That stuff works." Despite my initial reluctance I was swept up by the fervour. Father Moran had already said I was one of 'them', a heretic, so why shouldn't I find people of my own kind? One afternoon after school I went to Louise's place and her mother began teaching me about séances and the spirit world. It was fascinating. And tantalising. The thought of being able to contact Terry again gave me something to hope for.

So there we were, a few days later, all organised around the back of St John's Church. Mary-Kay had brought a scrabble set and a drinking glass to use as a Ouija board. We set the scrabble pieces out in a circle with the glass in the middle. "So who's going to do this?" Cassandra asked. "Marie should," said Louise. "It's her cousin and she's got the Devil in her already." Everyone was too nervous to laugh as we all put our fingers on the upturned glass. Then the girls realised that I couldn't ask the spirits anything without my voice, so Darlene asked the questions in my stead: "Is there anyone there? Are you there, Terry?" We glanced at each other anxiously. She tried again: "Terry, Marie just wants to know if you're okay?"

We sat there in silence as it happened. I didn't believe it at first but we all saw it - the glass seemed to rise up above the scrabble pieces. I blinked and rubbed my eyes. No, I wasn't hallucinating. Then, as I struggled to comprehend what was going on, the glass shattered in mid air. Thousands of tiny shards fell back to the ground.

Little did I know that while we were preparing for our séance, Ms Widdows was showing Sister Gerard the newspaper clippings about Terry and reminding her about the 'dream' I'd had a few weeks earlier. I have no doubt that Ms Widdows was simply concerned for me, and that she was trying to help, but she was a lay teacher, and in Catholicism things like that just didn't happen. Sister Gerard went straight to Father Moran, and things converged pretty quickly from there.

In the eyes of Father Moran it was the work of the Devil to have 'visions' and it was an act of evil to attempt to communicate with the dead. He was already convinced that God was punishing me for my sins by taking my speech from me, so it really didn't help matters when he found us behind the church, mid-séance.

All at once all hell broke loose.

Immediately after the glass from our Ouija board shattered Father Moran's voice boomed out behind me. I didn't know where to turn. I just heard the noise and the cursing, not the actual words. The girls were as confused as I was. We jumped up, each of us looking at the other, knowing we were in trouble, but not sure which direction the greatest danger was coming from.

The tennis racquet landed before I even saw it. I just felt the thud at the back of my head. To say Father Moran was 'ropeable' is too mild a word. He was already beetroot in colour and growing purpler by the second. I guess our senses were already heightened with the séance and the breaking glass, but with his long black dress coat and his thick rimmed glasses Father Moran literally looked larger than life. I was terrified. If the Devil himself had turned up at that minute I might have sought refuge with him.

Father Moran roared like thunder, and I swear I felt little lightning shocks all over my body. He struck the other girls with his racquet and sent them away with one of the sisters who had come out to see what all the commotion was about. Then, with my head ringing and not being really sure where I was, he grabbed me by the hair and dragged me around the church, up the steps and into the vestibule.

"You Whore of Babylon," Father Moran screeched. "How dare you take the innocent souls of my girls and sell them to the Devil?" His voice seemed louder than ever as his words reverberated off the stone walls of the church. "I always knew you were trouble," he went on. "Even before God saw fit to take your voice, and we all know he did that for good reason." I slumped against the wall as the yelling went on and on and on. "You will rot in hell for your evil," he shouted. "I know you're in collusion with Satan. How else could you know your cousin was going to die? How else could you speak with the dead?" With every accusation Father Moran pulled me up by my hair and then slammed me back down again. Finally, he let me fall to the floor. "Don't you dare come into the house of God ever again," he hissed as he turned away.

I had vomited. It was all over my clothes. I think I had wet myself too - my legs felt warm and wet. And the figure on the cross at the other end of the church was facing the other way. He did nothing to help me or to intervene.

If there had ever been any light at the end of the tunnel, now all became darkness. Courtney told one of the sisters that her grandfather was abusing her and she got the cane for 'lying'. Then I got the cane too, because I knew about it and that meant we were still seeing each other after they had told us not to.

Darlene's brother crashed his motorbike into a pylon and died. Father Moran officiated at the funeral, where he told Darlene because of her sins she was responsible for his death.

Then Cassandra was forced to have an 'internal examination' because Sister St Patrick accused her of becoming pregnant with Father Carr. She was still intact of course, but the damage was already done - her reputation was ruined.

I don't know exactly when I reached the point of no return. Maybe I would have put up with things for longer if it had just been me. Or maybe it was bound to happen after Father Moran dragged me into the church that day of the séance. Maybe it was the culmination of everything, like the straw that broke the camel's back. I don't know.

I wasn't hysterical. I didn't want to kill myself. But I'd had enough. I couldn't take anymore.

I remembered the pills that Louise had given me. I knew there would be bad days ahead when Louise might not be at school, so I'd saved most of them, storing them in an old bottle in my school bag where I knew no-one would find them. I hadn't imagined that one day, in the depths of despair, I'd be tempted to take them all at once. But now I thought of the comfort, of the peace and quiet. I thought of escape from a world where all is accusation and abuse, where maybe the Devil really did have me in his clutches, like Father Moron believed.

That afternoon I calmly made the decision and swallowed the pills with a glass of water from the staff room. Of course, I wasn't allowed in the staff room, but I didn't care - I wasn't planning on being awake when they found me.

As I waited for the pills to take effect I asked myself why Father Moran hated me so much. What had I actually done that was so bad? I racked my brain but I couldn't think of a valid answer. I'd only gone to the people who were supposed to help me. The only conclusion I could come to was that the God I'd always known, the Church I'd always believed in, had rejected me.

These were the thoughts I was thinking when Sister Kathryn found me in one of the lounge chairs in the staff room. She told me in no uncertain terms to get back to class but I didn't want to move, I was too lost in introspection. She yelled at me and struck me across the face but I didn't feel anything so she stormed off, saying she was going to fetch Father Moran. I was disappointed. The pills were taking too damn long to send me to sleep. Before Sister Kathryn could come back with Father Moran I forced myself to get up and I stumbled out into the middle of the road between St John's Church and St Anne's High School.

It seemed as good a place as any so I lay down on the road. I lay on my back and looked up. The sky was blue and the clouds were scattered around like little fluffy rugs. The road was warm and I could smell the tar. I wondered if it would melt and stick to my body. My thoughts meandered without reason. Lyrics that I'd never paid attention to before suddenly made perfect sense: 'Now it's just another show - you leave 'em laughing when you go. And if you care, don't let them know - don't give yourself away...'

I suppose time continued to pass but I no longer noticed it. The outside and the inside blurred together. I could hear my lost voice, loud and clear, singing 'Amazing Grace' in my head: '...save a wretch like meeeeee, I once was lost...' Maybe that's what I was, I thought; a lost wretch. In my vague state I wondered if anyone would bother to save me. Elvis? David Cassidy? No? Kurt Russell, yep he's the one - Kurt Russell will come flying around the corner any minute and whisk me away to America, the land of the freeeeee...

Random thoughts and songs continued to run through my head. 'I beg your pardon, I never promised you a rose garden, along with the sunshine there's gotta be a little rain sometimes...' What? I didn't even want a rose garden. A small shack on the beach would do, just for meeeeee... and maybe Kurt.

Soon I felt soothed, peaceful. Father Moran will have a lot of explaining to do, I thought sleepily. Whoever heard of anyone lying the middle of the road to stop the world from turning? I closed my eyes. It was quiet and nothing mattered anymore.

Then I was floating. Up, out of my body
Floating off, away, away from my grief
Out of consciousness.

Reality and imagination became one and the same and I thought I saw Terry in the darkness. I reached out for him but I couldn't touch him. At first I assumed he just hadn't seen me, but then he seemed to shake his head and he held his hand up. There was a rushing sensation and I felt myself falling away from him. There were voices in the background and there was a pounding in my ears. I felt sick. "Ouch, what are you doing, get your hands offa me... Leave me alone, just go away... Stop grabbing me..." I heard the words in my head, as if I was saying them, but I wasn't. I felt muddled. Everything seemed to be so far away.

I was lifted semi-conscious into an ambulance and when I came to I was lying in a crisp white hospital bed. I think it was the smell of disinfectant that woke me. A nurse with chubby cheeks was wiping my hair from my face. She had the voice of an angel. She said I'd tried to kill myself and she wanted to know why. I just looked at her, but she kept asking me questions in her sweet soothing voice. I tried to reach for a piece of paper to write on but she stopped me. "No dear, you don't need that," she said, "you can tell me anything..." Was it just the tone of voice she used, or was it that she called me 'dear'? I don't know what it was, to be honest, but all of a sudden I saw her turn into an ugly gargoyle. I had an overwhelming feeling that she would devour me but I felt too tired to run away. I turned over with my back to her and must have fallen asleep again.

A little later I was visited by the hospital social worker and there were more questions. "Where did you get the pills from? Did someone give them to you? Did you steal them?" I didn't answer. I didn't want Louise getting into trouble on my account. She'd only been trying to help me when she gave me her mother's 'happy pills'. She was just trying to cheer me up.

I tried to convince the social worker that I hadn't tried to commit suicide. It wasn't really death I'd wanted. It was simply a cry for peace, for an end to the war. But it didn't make sense to her the way it all made sense to me. I wanted someone to listen, to understand, but I knew how it looked.

Luckily the social worker didn't press me on the subject. Perhaps she was afraid of what I might do. Eventually she told me that they would let me go home as long as I agreed to continue seeing her as an outpatient. Sure, I thought, whatever you say - just let me out of here.

It was all a bit anticlimactic when I came home from the hospital. Denise looked at me oddly, but my parents didn't say much. I suppose they were probably in a state of shock, having been told that their daughter had attempted suicide. It can't have been easy for them but whatever they thought about it all they didn't give me a hard time - they'd been told to let me be and to carry on as 'normal', whatever that was...

CHAPTER 9

When I came home from the hospital I made it clear to my parents that I wouldn't go back to St Anne's. 'Not now, not ever,' I wrote, underlining the words several times. Mum conceded, but a couple of days later she asked me to put on my school uniform and to accompany her and Dad to the school for a meeting with the principal. I didn't want to go but Mum insisted. "Just this last time," she said, "to clear things up." I still felt like a beetle in a glass jar, but now I had a glimpse of the world outside - I was about to be released.

I could hear the murmur of voices in the classrooms as we walked through the grounds of St Anne's to Sister Gerard's office. It felt strange, a step away from reality - school life was continuing for all the other girls, but not for me. When Sister Gerard ushered my parents into her room for a 'talk' it was as though I was all alone in the middle of everything. Snippets of conversation drifted from behind the door of the principal's office but I zoned out as I waited outside. I didn't know what my parents or Sister Gerard were saying but I didn't care. I was just glad that no one was yelling at me or chastising me for once.

All of a sudden a shrill voice jerked me back to reality and the peace was shattered. "What do you think you're doing here? Get back to class this very minute!" I looked up to see Sister St Patrick, angling towards me. There was nothing I could do as she stormed on with all her usual abuse: "God has taken away your speech to punish you for your wrong doing...

You must repent... Obey the Lord's commands... Forsake the Devil before he takes you to hell..."

Sister St Patrick didn't know that Mum and Dad were in Sister Gerard's office and could hear everything she said. Dad came rushing out first. He stared at Sister St Patrick and I saw fury in his eyes. It's something I'll never forget. Then Mum appeared by his side and that was it. I don't know what Sister Gerard had been discussing with my parents but when they heard Sister St Patrick berating me they knew something of what I'd truly been subjected to at that school. We didn't stay a moment longer. Mum put an arm around me and we all walked out, leaving St Anne's forever.

I'm not sure my friends in the Elvis group really knew what happened to me when I left, but then I don't think any of them were fully aware of what I was going through during my final weeks at school. Towards the end the nuns had been determined to keep us separated, and I didn't seek them out as I would have liked because I didn't want them to get into the same trouble I was always in. I remember one day Darlene came to see me while I sat by myself on a bench in front of one of the classrooms. She asked why I didn't hang around with them anymore and I wanted to cry. I wanted to tell her that the Elvis girls were the only friends I had. I wanted to tell her that was nothing I wanted more than to be able to hang out with her and Mary-Kay, and Cassandra, Courtney, Marusia and Louise. Of course I didn't want to be isolated but at the same time I didn't want them to suffer the consequences of being seen with me. There was so much that I wanted to explain to Darlene, but before I could write anything down one of the sisters came by and shooed her away.

Some time later Mum received a letter from Sister Gerard, telling her not to worry about the school fees we owed. There was also a letter for me, wishing me the best. I didn't think much of it then but I have often remembered that letter in later years. Of all the nuns at St Anne's, Sister Gerard would have been one I would have liked to catch up with again. At the time I only saw her as a disciplinarian, but from her point of view the evidence was against me. She had no reason to disbelieve Father Moran and Sisters Kathryn and St Patrick, and with the three of them always rallying against me there was probably not much anyone could have done.

Looking back on it, I've often wondered how different my school life might have been if Father Carr had been pulling the strings, instead of Father Moran. I doubt that I would have ever gotten along with Sister St Patrick, but my relationship with Sister Gerard and the other sisters would certainly have been less strained. What would the future have held for me in that parallel universe? What opportunities would have presented themselves? What would my debutante's ball have been like? Once upon a time I even dreamed of going to university. But when I left St Anne's I was fifteen years old and I wasn't going back to school for anyone. My hopes of a higher education were dashed, just like that.

Questions about my future didn't occur to me until long after leaving St Anne's, however. Back then I had more immediate concerns to deal with, such as facing the consequences of my 'suicide attempt'. Before I'd left the hospital I had agreed to see the social worker again, and sure enough it wasn't long before she instructed my parents to bring me in for an appointment.

At first it seemed like just another interview with a disinterested doctor. The social worker stood in the background nodding as Mum, overwhelmed and only trying to help me, scrawled her signature on the forms that were pressed on her. I didn't know it at the time, but the forms gave the hospital the right to do what they thought best for me, even though no-one had made it clear what that was. It wasn't Mum's fault; doctors always knew best in those days, and you didn't ask too many questions, especially if you were a 'lowly housewife'.

Thinking about what happened next, the expression 'out of the frying pan, into the fire' springs to mind. Before I had even adjusted to leaving school I was locked away in the hospital's psychiatric ward. The doctor said I was safe and could rest there until my 'problems' were sorted out, but the psych ward was a whole new nightmare. No problems would be sorted out there, I realised, as I took stock of my new surroundings. So much for freedom from the glass jar. I felt like I'd been shaken out into gaol, a gaol in hell.

Men and women were bundled together in the one ward, with only thin curtains to separate the beds. There were no locks on the bathroom cubicles or toilet doors and toilet paper and sanitary pads had to be asked for. We were all jumbled together: drug addicts, self harm cases, nervous breakdown and serious disorder patients. And me.

The sounds and smells and sights of the psychiatric ward battered me and shattered me.

Being there made me want to creep further into myself, to get away from it all. But I couldn't get away and there was no such thing as privacy anymore. Every hour in the psych ward was accounted for. We had group therapy time, craft time and time with the counsellors. Then there were mealtimes and medication times. However you looked at it, there was no time to yourself at all. Even when we slept we weren't really alone - the mutterings and cries in the night put my teeth on edge. And then as well as the patients there were the nurses, the orderlies, the counsellors and the doctors. I'll never forget the sound of all those hard-soled shoes click-clicking on the floor tiles. There was never a moment's peace.

When Father Moran threatened me with 'punishment' he used to say I could be gaoled for heresy, which didn't make any sense to me. Heresy wasn't a word that was used much and I didn't really know what it meant, even when I looked up the definition. I had never willfully rejected God or the Church. But when I was admitted to the psychiatric hospital I thought that must be why I was there - because I was a heretic.

Mum was crying when she walked out of the hospital that morning but I just couldn't understand why she left me there. I could only assume that she and Dad agreed with the doctor, in which case they thought I was mad. Madness or heresy - there didn't seem to be much to choose between them, and either way there I was, exiled from everything I knew.

That first day in the ward I was told to have a shower and my vital statistics were taken for my medical records. Apart from the usual blood tests, however, there were no physical tests. No one thought to examine me for a physiological cause for my voicelessness. As for me, I didn't really know what was happening. I thought that the devil really was coming for me and I was halfway to hell already.

It wasn't until much later that I found out that my parents weren't aware of what was actually going on until it was too late. Mum did sign the admission papers but the doctor hadn't told her the whole story and there was no mention of keeping me there. He only said it was so they could help me. Neither Mum nor Dad had any idea what the psychiatric ward was actually like.

I'd only just escaped St Anne's but sure enough, the torture began all over again. Now my torturers weren't Father Moran or Sister St Patrick but rather the hospital counsellors. Day in, day out, session after session, they badgered me. They pressed me to tell them about my relationship with my parents, as they seemed to be sure that I'd suffered at their hands. They questioned me about the loss of my voice time and time again, demanding answers - answers that I simply could not give.

STOP IT.

IT'S NOT TRUE

NOTHING HAPPENED TO ME.
NOTHING. NOTHING.
NOTHING. IT'S ALL LIES.
LIES.

I want to scream the words but I can't. Whatever I write, however much I shake my head or refuse to agree, no matter if close my eyes or try to ignore them, they don't believe me.

They give me medication to 'calm me down', and they just keep on asking, pressing, probing, nagging, fishing, PUSHING for the answers they want to hear.

Slowly, slowly, the counsellors wear me down. They make me question myself and question my parents until I don't know what to think or feel anymore. Mum and Dad come to visit but I can't look at them. It's easier just to cut everything off, to go numb.

> Finally I give up.
> I give up trusting,
> I give up thinking,
> I give up fighting,
> I give up trying,
> I capitulate …
> I Surrender.

Dad brought chocolates. The chocolates reminded me of the Easter eggs that had been waiting for me when I first lost my voice. It had only been two years but already that Easter felt like a lifetime ago.

Mum said they loved me. But they let the doctor put me in this awful place, I thought; they *let* this happen to me. How could they do that if they loved me?

I didn't trust them anymore. I began to wonder if maybe they *had* abused me, as the counsellors had suggested. I know deep down that it wasn't the truth, but at the time it was as if the lines were blurring between what was real and what was imagined. I couldn't be sure of anything anymore.

The only good thing about the psych ward was that I made friends with Eric, the patient in the bed next to mine. I noticed Eric straight away because he wore a red baseball cap - he was the one splash of colour in the bleach-white world of the psych ward. The nurse told me not to get any ideas. She said Eric was too old for me, but there was nothing sexual about our relationship anyway; we were just friends who met in extraordinary circumstances. Eric was a recovering drug addict. I don't know which drugs he was addicted to but it wouldn't have mattered if I did, as I didn't know anything about drugs apart from my flirtation with the happy pills. I guess I was pretty naïve. Eric didn't look 'old' to me, but I never asked him his age - it seemed irrelevant.

On Saturday nights the common room of the psych ward would be done up for visitors. We had tea and coffee and nibbles, and we were allowed to play LPs from the ward's small record collection. Eric and I would get together and hog the turntable. There were quite a few nice songs in the record collection, but my favourite was 'Sealed with a Kiss' by Bobby Darin. Eric knew I liked it so he used to play it for me over and over, until he was told to stop. Then he would put it on one more time and we would dance. For me that was my graduation dance, because I didn't think I would ever have another one. Me and Eric, sealed with a kiss.

One day I started menstruating and didn't have any sanitary napkins. I went to the nurse with my pen and paper and asked her for some pads. "I'll have to check with the doctor first," she said. 'Please, I need them now,' I wrote. 'I've started already.' "No, I have to check with the doctor," she insisted. "Now go away before I call a wardsman, and you know what will happen if I do that." I went back to my bed in tears. I couldn't do anything to stop the bleeding, so I lay on the bed and tried to stem the flow with a towel.

Eric saw my distress and was furious. He ripped up a sheet and made a wad of material. Then he helped me clean up. He pulled the sheets off my bed and took them to the laundry for cleaning. But just at that time the nurse came in and saw what he was doing. She wasn't interested in his explanation. She called the wardsmen and told them that Eric was uncontrollable and needed to be put in the 'quiet room'.

The wardsmen swooped in. They pushed my bed out of the way and they punched Eric down to the ground. When he was down they continued punching and kicking him. Eric struggled but he was no match for two big orderlies. They were vicious. When he slumped over they picked him up and threw him onto his bed, where they hit him some more. By the time they brought the tranquilisers, there was no need for them. Eric was quiet and still and he didn't look like himself anymore. His red baseball cap lay disregarded on the blood-splattered floor tiles.

I crouched in the corner, hugging my knees, silent tears pouring from my face. I never saw Eric again after that but the way I saw it, he was beaten up for trying to help me. I felt terrible and I was afraid they would come for me next.

The next morning I overheard a nurse saying that they were putting me on the list for electroshock treatment. I'd seen them take patients for EST before - I'd heard them screaming all the way down the hall.

I knew I had to get out of there so I made a brazen plan. In the absence of anything better I decided that while everyone was distracted with visitors on Saturday night, I would simply walk out. And that's just what I did.

I waited until the end of visitor's hours that Saturday. Then, when the opportunity came, I picked up my bag and followed a family that were leaving. My pulse was racing but I had to force myself to walk calmly and naturally - step by step, moment by moment.

I didn't allow myself to look back. With each breath I had to override the panic that rose up like bile in my stomach. With every step I had to override the impulse to run from my prison, from electroshock 'therapy', from my name on 'the list'. My heartbeat was like a hammer inside me.

At any moment I expected to hear a shout, to see feet running after me, to feel a firm hand on my shoulder stopping me, turning me around, dragging me back the way I'd come. But I kept walking. I walked down the hallway from the psychiatric ward and into the main wing of the hospital. I walked through the overlit corridors, past the reception, and straight out through the main entrance, into the darkness outside. I was free!

Chapter 10

"One man's fault is another man's lesson," Nana used to say. I thought they were just words at the time, but now I can see that she was talking about context and attitude - an experience can either be positive or negative, depending on what we draw from it. It doesn't make a difficult experience any easier to bear, but it does give us a way to move forward, or to make sense of what we have been through. Then again, you need time to reflect on what you may have learned, and on the run from the psychiatric ward I wasn't exactly in a reflective frame of mind. All I wanted to do was escape!

At first I didn't believe I was free - I couldn't believe my plan had worked. I hurried away from the hospital in a euphoric daze, drunk on the fresh air of the night around me, and as my freedom sank in I wondered why I hadn't done it earlier. My escape gave me energy and confidence and as I looked up at the stars I had a glimpse of the possibility that I could turn things around. Finally, something was going right!

I headed down Crown Street, out of the city. I was aware of car lights flashing past me as I walked, but nothing much more. My heart was still racing, and my thoughts bounced around in my head. The farther away I got from the hospital the better I felt, but after a while I had to answer the question of where to go. My trust had been eroded. Mum and Dad might send me back to the hospital if I went home, I thought. So I decided to head for Sean's house in Warilla. I hadn't seen Sean and his sisters for a while but we'd all been friends since I had arrived in Australia. Our parents had met through the Shellharbour Workers' Club, and I felt sure his family would take me in now that I was in trouble. I'd be safe there.

With this in mind I moved on through Wollongong's industrial area, where the warehouses were lit up like Christmas trees and the cars flowed faster on the dual carriageway. I was pleased with my pace and the distance I'd already put between me and the psych ward. Taking a shortcut through the residential neighbourhood of Cringila seemed like a good idea at the time, but a passing taxi sent a warning shot of fear into my heart as it slowed down. I was a lone teenage girl, out in the middle of the night. What if I'd already been missed? What if there was an alert out and taxi drivers had been asked to help search for me? What if this taxi tried to pick me up, to take me back to the hospital? Or if he radioed the police?

I ducked up a side street, keeping to a suburban block where people were contained in their houses, doing the washing up, watching television, or already in bed. I did my best to keep a low profile but it wasn't long before I noticed a Holden station wagon drive past me, do a U-turn, and then drive back, this time a little slower. I felt my body tighten as the car rolled by that second time. I saw eyes peering out of the driver's window. There were only a few street lights and it was getting late.

My mind filled with dread as the car turned again and stopped somewhere behind me, engine running. A door opened and closed and then the car started moving again, slowly, slowly inching up alongside and then ahead of me. I glanced over my shoulder. One guy was behind me, slouching in my direction. Up ahead the station wagon stopped and another guy got out, turning to face me in the shadows. The squeal of the tyres as the car made another U-turn panicked me into action. I ran.

———

I run across a vacant lot,

Down one street, up another, over an Intersection, I can hear the car following,

I run and run,

My breath on fire,

My feet thumping on the pavement, Fear thumping in my chest, Catching in my throat,

I run, I run, I run...

I can hear the hum of the car drawing closer, closer. Light glimmers from one of the houses and I run towards it, almost choking on my ragged breath. I stagger through the gate and up the front stairs. I knock, knock on the door. My heart thumps in my ears as my knuckles knock, knock, knock and a voice from inside struggles to form words in English.

"Who there?

Who? Who?

What name?"

I scream it out:

"MARIE, MARIE, MARIE, PLEASE, PLEASE OPEN,

THEY'RE AFTER ME!"

But of course no sound comes from my mouth, just the rasping of my breath. I hear footsteps and the throb of the engine outside the gate behind me. I hear a male voice growl. "Come on girl, come with us; this isn't your house."

"Tell name please, tell," the woman's voice says again from inside. I knock harder on the door, I knock my urgency, my fear. I've never been so frightened, I try, I try, I try to find my voice.

"LOOK OUT THE WINDOW,

FOR GOD'S SAKE OPEN THE DOOR, PLEASE, PLEASE OPEN THE DOOR!"

Can she hear my soundless voice? Can she hear the pleading of my body and soul? Can she hear the danger in the purr of the engine of the car, crawling up and down the street? Behind me I hear the man growl again: "Come with us love, you know you don't live here."

Suddenly the door burst open and I was pulled inside. A small Asian woman and a teenage boy in pyjamas stood there, staring at me. I tried to explain myself but I was shaking so much that it was hard to find the pen and paper in my bag, and it was even harder to write anything down.

The boy's English was better than his mother's. Eventually I was able to make them understand what had happened. I didn't mention the hospital, of course, but they knew I was in trouble. It must have been so strange for them, having a mute girl arrive in a panic at their front door that night, but the woman made me a hot chocolate and when I had calmed down she drove me over to Sean's place. I guess she must have told me but I've never been able to remember her name, or even exactly where her house was. Still, I have never forgotten how she took me in when I needed help. Because of her I will always answer my door when someone knocks, even if I don't know who they are - it could be somebody just like I was, lost or in need of a helping hand.

I remember crying with relief when Sunny, Sean's mum, let me in. Sean just happened to be home on leave and we all sat in the lounge room while I explained what had happened. Sean had joined the Navy a year or so before this and in my naïvety I thought that I could maybe disappear with him when he returned to base. I told Sean and his mum how much I hated the hospital and how I didn't trust my parents anymore. I told them I was willing to do anything to start a new life.

Sunny went upstairs while Sean and I sat in the lounge room eating raisin toast. He put his arm around me and kissed me on the forehead, the way a big brother might. I felt understood, accepted. I thought my troubles were over. For the first time in ages I felt safe.

But it wasn't to last. While Sean and I were sitting together, Sunny was on the upstairs phone, calling the hospital. I didn't suspect anything when she joined us again, but it wasn't long before there was a knock on the door. I looked at the clock on the wall. It was after midnight. I looked over at Sunny but she wouldn't make eye contact. Sure enough, one of the hospital's nurses had come to get me.

Sunny said she had no choice. She said if I was her daughter she would want to know where I was, and she argued that my parents and the hospital staff must be worried. She said that she just wanted to do the right thing and she hoped that when I felt better I would understand. My eyes sank to the geometric patterns of the carpet at my feet as she spoke. I was beaten. I didn't fight, I just got up and followed the nurse out to the car.

The nurse assured me that I'd be okay but I thought it was all over. I thought they would sedate me and that I might never wake up again. I didn't believe her when she promised that the doctor would review my case in the morning and that my parents would come in and that everything would be alright. But I didn't have much choice. I'd seen how the orderlies operated. It was like something out of 'One Flew Over the Cuckoo's Nest'. If I didn't come willingly they might force me.

Back in the psych ward I stayed awake, despite my exhaustion. I was so sure that something terrible was going to happen to me that every sound set me on edge; the squeaks and the blips and the clatter of the hospital and the human noises too. At one point I must have eventually dozed off because I awoke with a start - in my subconscious terror I had wet the bed.

The next morning my parents came to see me, just as the nurse had promised. At first I suspected a trick when we were all interviewed in the doctor's office. I thought things were bound to get worse so I couldn't believe my ears when I heard the doctor apologising. He said it had been a mistake, that I shouldn't have been left in the hospital. He said he had been out of town and had only just realised I was still there.

The doctor went on to say that there was nothing psychologically wrong with me except for depression, which was to be expected at my age, especially in the wake of having lost my voice and my experiences at St Anne's. He said there had been no reason to keep me in the psychiatric ward, and he was angry that I had been there so long. But how could he not have known? I was numb. I didn't know who to trust or what to believe anymore. I didn't buy that it had all been a 'mistake'. I had been kept in the psych ward for weeks. I had been put on the list for EST, for God's sake. I had seen my friend Eric beaten to a pulp by the hospital staff.

When Mum and Dad took me home I just wanted to be alone. After everything that had happened I didn't want anything to do with people for a while, them included. The term hadn't yet been coined, but I suppose I was suffering from a form of post traumatic stress. I pulled the curtains closed and played my copy of the Bee Gees' 'Saved by the Bell' over and over again. I hid under the sheets and spent my days in bed. I needed time.

As my bedroom was next to the lounge room, I often heard Mum and Dad talking at night. They didn't yell or raise their voices but recriminations were frequent, and I often heard Mum crying. "I should have known, it wasn't right to keep her in that place," she said one night, her voice breaking. "We shouldn't have left her there Danny, we should have taken her away!" Dad's voice was quieter than Mum's and he didn't have so much to say, but Nana was often quick to talk over both of them. "That girl will be the death of you, she needs sorting out, and quick," I heard her say. I could almost see her through the wall, shaking her head with disapproval as she spoke.

Nana had come out from the UK to stay with us. With Mum still working long hours at the pub Nana thought someone should be around to keep an eye on me, especially after I left school. So she was wrong about me never seeing her again, but sometimes I wished she'd been right. As soon as she moved in with us she seemed to spend most of her time putting me down. She chastised me for upsetting Mum, and she often told me how much I needed a good belting. Sometimes I'd go to bed fully clothed, just in case Dad listened to her and I had to make a run for it. Dad was a gentle man but even his patience could be tried.

Most nights the conversations went on and on, and because of where my bed was situated it was like a funnel - I could hear everything. "There's something not right with her, Veronica," Dad said to Mum. "Maybe we should take her to another hospital for more tests?" My heart sank into my stomach. Thankfully, Mum refused, and in a rare moment of solidarity she was backed up by Nana: "We should sue them for what they've done," she said. "They could have ruined her for life."

I sometimes wonder what became of my fellow patients in that psychiatric ward, and I also wonder how many of them, like myself, shouldn't have been there in the first place. I suppose that things have improved since those days - we don't tend to just lock people up in psych wards anymore and the use of electroshock therapy is considerably more regulated. But it took me a long time to regain any trust in the medical profession, and the fear of hospitals that the experience fixed in me is still with me today.

CHAPTER 11

My experience in the psychiatric ward really changed my outlook on life. Before leaving St Anne's I thought that I would be fine out in the real world, but now I realised that things weren't as I had imagined. The real world didn't care for me anymore than Father Moran cared for me at school. And now that I was seen as a failed suicide case I felt more ostracised than ever. I looked at everyone and everything with a new level of distrust. All I wanted was to be alone in my bedroom.

When I came home from the hospital I was miserable for a long time. I began to expect the worst of everyone and I became cynical. I acted with a mean spirit before others could have the chance to be mean to me. The only exception was my friend Courtney, who stuck by me, thick or thin. Courtney was still at St Anne's but we would catch up on weekends and she would sometimes sleep over at my house. Thank God for Courtney, because other than her I pushed everyone away that year. It was a kind of self-defence, I guess, but I'm not proud of it. In hindsight I was a terrible teenager, despite the difficulties I faced. Who knows how much worse I might have been without Courtney to confide in?

My poor parents suffered the worst of it. I remember staring at Dad one evening and thinking 'I could easily hit you in the back of the head with a hammer, and it would be over for you'. Of course I would never actually do anything like that, but the thought was a reflection of how desperately unhappy I was. I'd confess these thoughts to Courtney but she would always laugh it off. "You're just a little down today," she'd say, and off she'd go to buy us ice creams. Courtney was a great friend, for sure, but the reality was that she wasn't always around. She had her own life to live. And meanwhile I was very often 'down' and I continued to feel trapped by my situation.

The problem was that I blamed the world for all my difficulties; I blamed the world for my inability to relate to people and for the fact that I felt that my parents didn't love me. It seemed to me that I was stuck in some kind of indefinite 'purgatory' and that I would never be set free, but rather than trying to improve things I wallowed in my misery and resentment. I probably wasn't much different from any other teenager in this regard, but lacking a voice made it all the more frustrating. I would take it out on my parents by ignoring them or refusing to go places with them, or I would stay in the car when we did go out together. It must have been pretty disheartening for them.

Despite all this, however, I still craved company and I wanted to be a good person. I certainly didn't want to feel ostracised and isolated, no matter how much I resented the world. As a naturally social person, the dearth of good relationships created a vacuum in my life. I guess the difference between me and every other teenager was that I couldn't even say a simple 'hello' if I wanted to. Something was missing, something wasn't right, and when Courtney wasn't around I didn't know how to fix it.

Mum arranged for me to start at Kiama High at the start of the new term, but I only lasted one day. I was still carrying the trauma of St Anne's and the psych ward with me and it was too soon for me to reconsider school. In truth, I was overwhelmed by the goodwill at Kiama High. I couldn't bring myself to trust the way the students and the teachers actually talked to each other as human beings. My would-be classmates were all friendly and curious, but I'd lost my faith in people. I didn't believe anyone would be nice to me without a hidden agenda.

The principal at Kiama High buddied me up with a girl called Angela. As we left his office he told her not to lead me astray and she laughed. I was thrown. This was contrary to what I knew - a principal with a sense of humour! Angela was kind and didn't seem put out at all by my voicelessness. She treated me like a real person. The trouble was that I wasn't used to being treated like a real person. It was all too much for me. I told myself that something was wrong. Why were they all being so friendly and helpful? Was it all a cruel joke? Were they trying to make me slip up, to do something wrong? Was I still being watched? Please, please, I thought - just let the day end so I can go home.

I caught the school bus back to Shellharbour and that night I told my parents I couldn't stay on at Kiama High. I really wanted to - I wanted to be part of 'something' again, but I just wasn't ready for it. So that was that. I was back home for good.

With Mum and Dad working so hard I was often at home by myself. Nana stayed with us for a few months and Denise was around after school, but otherwise it was just me. Most days I did the housework and prepared dinner as I didn't have anything better to do. Occasionally I'd go out to the shops, but that was the extent of my public interaction.

Back then we didn't have big supermarkets. We did the family shopping in Shellharbour Village. Mum made the same order each week at the butcher, the fruit and veg shop, and the little corner store that sold all the other regular groceries. One day I went to that store to pick up some bread and on the way home a boy smiled at me as I waited to cross the road. I recognised Charles Ennis, who I had gone to primary school with, before starting at St Anne's. "Hi Marie, nice to see you," Charles said. He looked around, as if to see if anyone was watching, and then went on. "I always liked you, but we're not allowed to talk to you," he said. I blinked. What did he mean, 'not allowed'? "Mum and Dad are friends with Dr Michaels," Charles explained. "He said everyone should avoid you because you're mad."

I know Charles meant well but this experience just reinforced my sense of isolation. Being reminded that everyone thought I was crazy didn't exactly help bring me out of my shell, so after that I avoided contact with anyone outside my own family. It was a time of more or less complete withdrawal in my life. I felt desperately lonely but there was something almost strangely comforting about it. Maybe it was a case of 'better the devil you know'. In any case, I stayed in my room most of the time, with only the radio and the television for company.

In those days we had an old laundry outside in the backyard. We washed our clothes in an ancient washing machine that we filled up with water from a hose attached to the cold tap. The clothes were rinsed the same way, by holding the hose over the drum while it was spinning. Then there was the hard yakka of feeding the garments through the roller to squeeze out the excess water. You had to be careful your fingers didn't get caught.

One day our landlord came by and saw me hanging out the washing. He said said that if a young girl like me was bunking school she should at least be on the beach with her friends, having fun, not stuck at home doing the housework. He meant well but I just stared at him. How could he possibly understand?

In the end it was my love of the movies that motivated me to get out and about more often. I loved films. I loved the music and all the people that were in them; not just the stars themselves, but the friendships that their characters had with each other. I wanted friendships like that. Having been isolated for so long I was sick of being alone. I hadn't even seen Courtney for a while, and I missed having her around to hang out with. Hollywood fantasies are all very well but I wanted someone real to care for, to share secrets with. I wanted a boyfriend. Puberty was taking its time catching up with me, but it was on the horizon...

I especially liked Elvis and Frankie Avalon films. One day, one of Mum's friends told me that I looked like Annette Funicello, which I thought was cool. She said it was because of my nice dark eyes and hair. What? I had nice eyes? I'd never noticed. I went into Mum's room and sat on her bed, staring into the mirror. Michael Jackson's 'Ben' was playing on the radio and I felt an odd kind of kinship with Ben, even if he was a rat and even if he did turn evil in the film of the same name.

I'd never really looked at myself like this before. At St Anne's we weren't allowed to be vain, so the few mirrors that were around were just to check that everything was 'in place'. But now that I was paying attention I realised Mum's friend was right, my eyes weren't too bad. My hair had grown long and curly, and I didn't know what had happened to the puppy fat I'd had, but it seemed to have moved itself into different places. I was growing up. I looked like a young woman. I might even be able to wear a bikini.

Despite the debacle at the psychiatric ward I still had to see a social worker once a week, but after I got over my reluctance it became something I really looked forward to. My newly assigned social worker, Helen, was lovely. She would take me for a drive, or to the shops where we would have an ice cream or a soft drink, and she would tell me about her day. When she told me about what was happening in her life she always focussed on the good things. She said that I had to find good things to focus on too, and she taught me that there is always something good in each day, even on a bad day.

Eventually another warm Australian summer came around. I started spending more time outside and less time in my bedroom. I sunbaked in the backyard, playing music and pretending I was at the beach, not by myself at home. Meanwhile, thanks to Helen, I started to notice 'good things' in my life. The most obvious good things were Courtney, of course, and my music and the movies I loved. But there were other things too. I realised that despite Nana's hard words, she still looked out for me, and she even bought me teen magazines from time to time, despite her aversion to them. So that was another good thing, wasn't it?

I still find something 'good' in every day, so that time with Helen really did leave me with something of value. But soon enough Helen was moved on to another position and I was assigned another social worker.

This new social worker told me to call her Sister Jackson. I never learned her first name.

I don't know how much Sister Jackson knew about my time at St Anne's but she was definitely a bad fit for me - she was the total opposite of Helen. Her idea of being my social worker was to sit me in the reception area outside her office for hours while she did whatever she did inside. Most of the time I just sat there, dreaming of the day I would turn sixteen and could leave her behind.

On one of the rare occasions that Sister Jackson actually spoke to me, she suggested I should go to a group called 'Grow'. Grow was a mental health self-help group that met every Tuesday night in Wollongong. Sister Jackson said that they met to talk about their problems and to help each other to cope.

I didn't trust Sister Jackson and I didn't want to go to Grow, but she gave me no choice. "Young lady, it's for your own good," she said. I stared blankly at her. "Someone needs to get through to you," she continued. "You're rude and aggressive and totally uncontrollable." I didn't know how she could think this of me as we hadn't really communicated with each other at all before this point. This was the longest 'conversation' we had in fact had. I suspected she knew Father Moran or one of the sisters at St Anne's because it seemed to me that even though I kept a low profile, I still got in trouble with her. I wished that Helen was still around. In any case, Sister Jackson talked with Mum and convinced her that I should go to Grow. So off I went into Wollongong. Once a week. To Grow.

CHAPTER 12

After many months of isolation I finally started to interact with other people again. It wasn't easy at first, but after a while I realised that not everybody had it in for me. Okay, so not everyone was my friend, but equally not everybody was my enemy. I eventually began to understand that most people are just doing their own thing, struggling with their own trials and tribulations. And some of them, despite whatever they may themselves be facing, still find the strength to help and look out for others.

As it happened I did make friends with a few of the members of Grow. My favourite among them was Dennis - he was a few years older than me and was a really nice guy. Even though our conversations were mostly one sided, he didn't seem to mind. He drove me home after the meetings, as he lived close by, and he chatted all the way, telling me about his girlfriend Desiree, and about his life and aspirations. He said that if I ever needed help I could call him. He said he would know it was me because of the silence and he would come over to my place. He was very protective and he reminded me a bit of Eric, from my time in the psych ward.

Grow sessions always opened with a prayer, which I bristled at. I didn't know what they would do about it, but I refused to close my eyes. I wasn't going to close my eyes for anyone. No one really minded though. The group convenor said that they weren't religious anyway; they just ran along with the same twelve step program that was made famous by Alcoholics

Anonymous. He said that prayer was just a part of that process and that for most people it seemed to help.

Things were okay at Grow but there was one guy in the group who really laid into me one time. I guess he'd had a bad day but he went ballistic - he said that I was no use to anyone, that I never participated in the group session, and that I might as well have been a ghost. That was a new one - no one had called me a ghost before. I must have looked upset because Dennis tried to comfort me on the way home that night. When he dropped me off he gave me a kiss on the forehead; a brotherly kiss just like the one Sean gave me when I ran away from the hospital.

Dennis got married a little while after I met him. When he invited me to the wedding I was over the moon. I planned what I would wear and I saved up to buy him and Desiree a nice present. But on the day itself I was overcome with a strange feeling. I couldn't go to the wedding, I just couldn't step outside my house. I thought I might feel better that evening, so I skipped the ceremony itself and when it was getting dark I asked Mum to call me a taxi to take me to Oak Flats, where the reception was being held.

I paid the taxi driver and got out at the address of the reception, but I still felt strange. It turned out that the driver had dropped me off around the back of the building so I walked around, looking for a way in. Eventually I found a side entrance but I stopped at the doorway, listening to the music and the people laughing and singing. I wanted to join them but I stood at the entrance for a long time, somehow unable to venture inside. It was as if I didn't know how to take part in such happiness, as if I could only be an outsider, looking in. I watched Dennis dancing with Desiree and was overcome by how beautiful they looked together. The song 'Hooked on a Feeling' by Blue Swede was playing when Desiree finally saw me and came over. "Marie, what are you doing out here?" she asked. I was mortified. But I convinced her that I had only just arrived when she asked how long I'd been standing there.

Desiree asked me to come inside, but I made some excuse about a family issue and pretended I had just dropped by to congratulate them.

Desiree called Dennis over and I did my best to hide my turmoil and appear upbeat when they both hugged me. Dennis said we would catch up later. As I turned to leave I realised that I would have to walk all the way home, as the taxi had long gone. Why did I do that, I asked myself. Why did I push away people that I like? I knew Dennis and Desiree were my friends and that they wouldn't hurt me. They only meant me well. So why couldn't I celebrate with them? Why did I have to run and hide?

It was classic self-sabotage, but looking back on it I'm not surprised. My self-esteem had been shot to pieces by my experiences at school and in the hospital, and I had grown accustomed to believing that I didn't deserve to enjoy life. At the time, though, I didn't understand it at all. All I knew was that I felt miserable and confused. As I walked away I could hear Peter Shelley's song 'Love me, Love my Dog'. I felt sorry for myself.

It was at one of the Grow meetings that I met Mark, although I'm not sure why he was in the group. He didn't actually say what his problem was but he had a pleasant manner and I felt more at ease with him than I did with most of the others. Mark noticed that I cringed and wouldn't close my eyes during the prayer at the beginning of the session. He asked me if it was because I didn't believe in God or if it was because of a bad experience. I thought he was very perceptive.

Mark told me he went to a church that didn't persecute people with different beliefs. He said it was a very open community where people simply cared for each other because they were human beings. It all sounded so welcoming, and Mark was clearly a nice guy. That's how I found myself going along with him to the Spiritualist Church.

Since I had left school there had been a few occasions when I had needed to attend the Catholic Church, such as for my sister Denise's confirmation. I went along but I found I just couldn't enter the buildings themselves - I'd feel nauseous and sometimes would even vomit. I guess after everything Father Moran said, I still believed that if I entered a church

I would be punished. They had conditioned me well at St Anne's. I felt as if I had to hide from God and not let him see me. I had to let Him forget I was here.

We still lived in Shellharbour at the time, three houses up from St Paul's Anglican Church. I used to walk past that church nearly every day but I would never go inside. On Sundays I would go to the shop to collect the newspaper and milk when the church service was on so I could hover outside and listen if they were singing hymns, but I was careful not to let anyone see me. I couldn't explain to them why I was so reluctant to enter.

Someone must have told the minister at St Paul's because one Sunday he came out and asked me to come inside with him. He offered me his hand and said it would be alright. He said I could just stay for a little while if I wanted. I really wanted to go with him but I couldn't; I was still convinced that I didn't belong. I don't think I met the minister's eye that day; I just backed away and hurried home.

I saw that minister several times over the next year or two. He was always very nice to me even though I never knew his name. He would often be outside the church, gardening or doing maintenance, and he would wave and call hello if he saw me passing by. On one occasion he helped carry my shopping bags back to the house for me. I think he was maybe the first contact I had in those days that would eventually bring me back to Christianity, years later, but at the time I believed that my case was hopeless. I was convinced that no matter how I tried I would never be a good enough person to go to heaven.

Meanwhile, thanks to Mark, I became more involved in the Spiritualist Church. I was wary of any mention of God (the Spiritualist Church is still a Christian denomination) but all the other stuff they talked about got my attention, and I had heard that Elvis was into spiritualism too. I was fascinated by their openness to séances and messages from the 'other side', and I wanted to know more about spiritual healing and spirit guides. Each month there was a guest speaker, and they regularly ran courses on any subject that was connected to the spirit world. I eagerly soaked everything up. The Spiritualist Church taught me that 'orthodox' churches were misleading in their teachings. They argued that God was not an angry old man with a stick, as was the common perception. They claimed that he was actually benevolent and approachable, and that we could talk to Him whenever we needed to.

When they learned about what had happened at St Anne's the Spiritualist Church community assured me I wasn't evil. They said that everyone had a gift and that I would find mine. They encouraged me to explore my spirituality and taught me to meditate, to open my mind let my spirit guide 'lead me in the right direction'. I was intrigued but I found this process very difficult. Firstly, I would always find my thoughts drifting or replaying events that I had experienced. Secondly, I didn't like the idea of an unknown entity entering my mind - I wanted to remain in control. I did try to keep myself open to the possibility, but in the end I never found my spirit guide.

I was better at taking part in the healing services, where members of the Spiritualist Church would pray whilst hovering their hands over your body. They wouldn't physically touch you but sometimes there was a sensation of warmth. It was after one of these services that a woman from the congregation approached me to say she had a message for me from 'beyond'. "It's a lady," she said. "She's close to you... but she's not close." She said the lady would 'pass over' soon, but that I should not be upset as it was a good thing - her body was tired and she was ready to go. I was confused and a bit scared. Someone who was close to me but not close? Tired and ready to go? What sort of riddles where these? What was the point of getting a message from the other side if I couldn't understand it?

The congregation at the Spiritualist Church reminded me of my Aunt Mary in Bolton. She was known as a 'gifted' woman. It was said that when she sat with people in pain, they would feel better. She didn't do anything theatrical, she just sat with them, sometimes holding their hands. People called for her so often that the local community gave her a telephone, so she could be reached quickly, and they also paid for the use of a taxi whenever she went to see people in need.

To me she was just Aunt Mary, Mum's sister. She had four children including Paul, who was around the same age as me, and she made the best steak puddings ever. Her hair had never fully recovered from the accident she'd had as a girl in the cotton mills, but other than that there didn't seem to be anything unusual about her. She spent her days like the rest of the women of Bolton: cooking, cleaning, and looking after her kids. But on top of that she visited people who were sick. When I was young, Aunt Mary told me that she had a special gift from God; somehow she was able to help people control their pain. She told me she didn't understand it fully, but it was God that did the work anyway - she was just the medium. She said a person with gifts such as hers had to be very diligent and had to keep God close to them. That was why she went to Mass every morning and was blessed by the priest. She said she was telling me all this because one day I would understand what she was saying.

Shortly after the woman from the Spiritualist Church gave me her 'message' I heard that Aunt Mary was dying of breast cancer. The news was particularly hard on Mum, who felt torn between spending time with her sister and looking after me and Denise. In the end Mum stayed with us and Nana returned to England to be with Aunt Mary during her final days. It was a sombre time, and when Mary died a few months later I knew that the world had lost a wise and compassionate woman. In my heart I asked for her to stand by me through my life and to meet me at Heaven's gates when the time finally comes.

Others might have been scared off but I felt comfortable at the Spiritualist Church, and I grew to trust the community that congregated there. Their séances weren't like the one I had tried with my friends at school. These were 'different'. I saw things that couldn't be explained and I was given information about myself that no-one else could possibly have known. I had no doubt that some of the congregation were highly 'gifted' and I craved more knowledge. For some Christians the word 'spiritualist' holds negative connotations but for me their Church served a positive purpose - I was interacting with people again and feeling a little bit better about my life.

CHAPTER 13

When I turned sixteen Mum took over the milk bar opposite the Shellharbour Workers' Club. She had saved up all her tips over the years and had been keeping a little bit aside from the extra hours she worked at the pub. It still wasn't enough to buy the business, but the little old ladies who sold the milk bar to her agreed to let her pay off the rest in installments. After sitting around at home for months I had the urge to 'do something' and it made sense to work for Mum. She didn't make enough money to pay me, but giving her a hand helped me feel like I wasn't just a burden on our family.

At first I wondered how I would cope, serving people without a voice. But Mum was around to keep things in check and I don't remember it being too much of an ordeal once I got over my apprehension. I made a lot of hamburgers, toasted sandwiches, and milkshakes. After a while the customers got to know me and everything was fine. I did everything a shop assistant normally does, except for the talking.

As a rule, I wouldn't serve strangers, as they'd get confused by my silence. Sometimes they thought I was a new Australian who just hadn't learned English. But it didn't take long for regular customers to get to know my situation and then it became easy to take their orders, because they could ask for what they wanted and I could either nod or shake my head, depending on how many meat pies were in the oven, for example, or how many hamburgers we had left. I must have done okay, because after a while I even had my own 'clientele' who would specifically wait for me to serve them.

Bit by bit, I slowly gained confidence at the milk bar. When I realised that some people actually wanted to have a conversation with me, I became quite good at 'mouthing' my words. I had to practice with the Australian accent, though - I had to shape my mouth differently to 'pronounce' the 'aaaaay' of the Australian alphabet, as opposed to the quick 'ah' of the Queen's English.

As I started getting to know people at the milk bar, I developed a few quirky relationships. One of these was with a delivery driver for Coca-Cola. He was quick with a smile and if I wasn't around he would leave me little notes. 'How ya goin mate? Missed ya this arvo!' - that kind of thing. They were such simple gestures, but they made my day. Slowly, ever so slowly, I started coming back to life, and as I gained courage I started venturing out more. I even managed to go shopping and ask for what I wanted by pointing to things. I was surprised to find that people in general were actually quite helpful. Things were starting to look up. Now I just needed to find some new friends!

The main street of Shellharbour ran between the milk bar and the Workers' Club, but the town wasn't so developed in those days and there were still several plots of dairy land dotted around. One day I was serving some local teenagers when a cow casually strolled over and stopped on the road outside. At the same time, a very happy man came out from the club, singing away to some song in his head. When he saw the cow the man stopped dead in his tracks, rubbed his eyes, and then turned and walked straight back into the club again. It was like a scene from a cartoon, and we all thought it was hilarious. I guess there must be some truth to the idea that comedy breaks down barriers because the teenagers asked me to join them at the beach that afternoon.

It became a regular thing that summer. I would finish at the milk bar around 3.30pm and then head to the beach or the pool to join my new mates. I didn't swim; I just sat there and listened to them chatting. Sometimes I would join in but it depended on the speed of the conversation. Often, by the time I had finished writing a comment in my notepad, they were already onto the next topic.

It was while I worked at the milk bar that I started going out with Lindsay, my first date. He was one of the local boys, blonde haired and very Australian, or 'Strine' as he would have pronounced it. Accent aside, Lindsay was quite a catch. To say I was gobsmacked would be an understatement, but in actual fact it happened really easily. One afternoon Lindsay asked me if I wanted to go to the movies and I simply gave him the thumbs up.

So there it was, I was going on my first real date. And sure enough, as soon as Lindsay walked out of the milk bar, the worries started. What if he kissed me? I didn't know how to kiss, not properly. I hadn't done it before, not unless I counted trying to kiss the picture of David Cassidy on my bedroom wall. Courtney showed me how to practice on my arm, but it wasn't the same so in the end I gave up. What was it Nana used to sing? 'Que sera, sera - whatever will be, will be'. Such a catchy song. Anyway, Lindsay might forget to kiss me. Or maybe I could keep him talking so he wouldn't be able to get around to it...

Lindsay and I went to see 'Jaws' at the Gala cinema in Warrawong. I wouldn't have gone if I'd known what we were going to watch. He didn't know about my fear of sharks but it turned out it was the third or fourth time he'd seen the film, and he told me when the bad bits were coming up so I wouldn't get frightened. I couldn't tell if it was because he was a gentleman, or because he didn't want to wear the coke I was nervously holding, but either way I felt cosy and comfortable with his arm around me, and I closed my eyes whenever I heard that classic two note theme build up from the bassline. After the movie we got a taxi home because we missed the bus. Lindsay walked me to my front door and smiled sweetly when he thanked me for the date. Then I leaned towards him and it happened without thinking; kissing wasn't so difficult after all!

One of my favourite memories with Lindsay was when the 'Show' came to town and we went to check it out with Courtney and her boyfriend Warren. Warren was quite a marksman on the shooting ducks and the laughing clowns, and Courtney ended up with several stuffed toys that he won for her. We ate cotton candy and 'Dagwood Dogs' and Lindsay somehow managed to sneak us a bottle of wine from the bar. Later that night there was a concert with Jon English and Air Supply. It was the first time I had seen Jon English up close - previously I'd only seen him on 'Countdown' or Donnie Sutherland's 'Sounds' program.

Lindsay and I never really got past the kiss and cuddle stage, but that was fine. We had nice times together without it getting complicated. I stayed in touch with him over the years and later on we'd always have a dance together if I saw him at the clubs on Friday or Saturday nights.

Around this time I heard a radio advertisement for Susie Elelman's modelling agency. I had always envied the models in women's magazines, and Susie herself had been a Miss Australia finalist a couple of years earlier. According to Susie's advert you would gain self- confidence, grace, and a knowledge of makeup techniques at her modelling course. It really appealed to me, because even though I had started trying to 'fit' into normal life, I still felt inadequate and thought I needed something to boost me up. I wrote to Susie, because I couldn't telephone, but I didn't receive a reply. After some time I became a little disheartened and I told myself I wouldn't have made a good model anyway - I was too short and I blushed too much.

Then, one morning in the milk bar, I was busy serving a customer when I heard a female voice asking for me. I looked up and nearly fell over: Susie might not have answered my letter but she had actually come to see me herself. And with her was Michael McRae, the newsman from WIN Television. Susie knew what she was doing - she knew how to create a sensation. And so it was that I embarked on a short lived but propitious modelling career.

As Susie's course was in Wollongong I had to travel by myself for the first time since being at school. I wrote 'Wollongong please' on a piece of card, and on the reverse side I wrote 'Shellharbour please'. I put the card in a plastic sleeve and kept it with me every time I caught the bus to attend

Susie's course. I got a few funny looks from the bus drivers at first, but they soon got used to me.

After a while I found that I actually enjoyed catching the bus. It gave me a sense of freedom that I hadn't had before. Prior to this I had relied on Mum, who would speak for me. If I'd had to go somewhere by myself I always walked. Now I found I could travel anywhere I wanted, as long as I wrote my destination down in advance. It was my first taste of independence, and to this day I still enjoy taking a bus ride.

Right from the start I felt comfortable with Susie. I completed the six or eight weeks of training and didn't come out of it too badly. I was still very shy, but was now aware that I had exactly the same fears about my figure as every other woman. Susie was a real mentor and it seemed to me that she took more than just a professional interest in my well-being, although that could just be wishful thinking on my part. In any case, she arranged for me to have a complete makeover. At that time my hair was very long and curly and some days it would even fall into ringlets, which I hated as they reminded me of Shirley Temple. Susie took me to her hairdresser, where I was given a contemporary cut and shown how to blow dry, which I had never done before. Then came the makeup. I'd worn lipstick a few times but beyond that I'd never really known what I was doing. Now I learned how to work with what I had and I discovered that earthy colours were best suited to my complexion. Susie said that makeup was meant to enhance a woman's natural beauty, not paint over it.

You wouldn't think that a small thing like visiting the hairdresser or fixing your makeup would make such a big difference in a girl's life, but it did for me - it made me feel good about myself. All of a sudden I felt grown up, and other people noticed the difference too. "Oh, you look so pretty," one of the ladies told me at the milk bar. "You've gotten rid of your little girl hair and emerged as a beautiful butterfly."

In all the years since, I've rarely met anyone with such enthusiasm as Susie. Under her tutelage we learned about everything from etiquette when out for important dinners, to what to wear in a bar. She was a powerhouse.

At the end of the course she even organised a fashion parade, with a proper catwalk. It was much more fun than actual modelling, which I found to be tedious and a bit stressful. In fact, by the time I realised I wasn't really cut out for a modelling career, it no longer mattered - Susie's course had worked wonders for my self- esteem.

In the end the milk bar only lasted a year. The two little ladies that had sold Mum the business didn't tell her about the proposed Shellharbour bypass. When the highway was completed the truckies didn't stop to buy their lunch or grab a cold drink anymore, and car drivers just sped past on their way north or south. Holidaymakers still dropped in if they were in town, but Shellharbour wasn't 'en route' anymore, and the milk bar, along with most of the small businesses in town, went bust.

It was actually good timing, as our landlord then decided he wanted to sell the house we had been living in, and he only gave us two weeks to move out. Dad wasn't impressed. He went to the Housing Commission to try to find us a new place, but they were reluctant to help, even though we had been on the waiting list since we had arrived in Australia.

Dad wasn't a violent man, but he was upset at the thought of his family being left homeless. At that time the government didn't help people in rental homes, and Dad was overcome with the shame of it. He got into a big argument at the Commission and they finally relented, offering us a house in Benaud Crescent, in Warilla. We hadn't seen the house but there were no other options so Dad just took it.

Mum liked Shellharbour, and didn't want to move to Warilla. She thought the suburb had a bad name, and for years afterwards when people asked her where we lived she would still say Shellharbour. But I liked the paisley curtains in my new room, and I thought Warilla had its merits. There was an atmosphere about the place. There were always kids playing in the streets and neighbours sat outside on summer evenings, having a beer after work. There was a community.

Those were the days when neighbours still looked after each other. If you saw someone you didn't know hanging around the street you would ask them if they needed help. If one of the kids was playing up and giving lip, they would get a wallop and told to run off. Adults simply had the last say, and if we complained that Mrs so-and-so had done this or that to us, we just got in trouble again because we had obviously been disrespectful.

I don't know what they made of me when we first moved to Warilla. Mrs Spratt, who lived down the street from us, used to call me Dumbo (no, not because I had big ears), but overall I was accepted like everybody else. I don't think the neighbours were even aware of why I couldn't speak. As far as I know it was never talked about, so at least I was free of the gossip of Shellharbour, where everyone knew me.

From Warilla, Mum and I would sometimes travel up to Sydney to watch the Mike Walsh Show or Blankety Blanks being filmed. We'd catch the bus in Wollongong and be dropped off in the city for some shopping and a bite to eat before heading to the TV station. It was a nice day out.

I found it interesting to see how TV shows were filmed. I hadn't known they were so staged, even to the point of telling the audience when to clap, or laugh, or look hostile. But it was fun. The best bits for me were when the entertainers came on. I got to see lots of singers and other performers, some of them even before they became famous. I particularly remember Jon English and Trevor White from Jesus Christ Superstar, and Pam Ayers, the English poet.

On one of these trips I was sitting with Mum in front of another lady and her daughter. All the way to Sydney and back the daughter did nothing but moan and complain. She complained about everything, from the bus being uncomfortable to the show being pathetic. It was embarrassing, the way she spoke to her mother. She yelled and swore at her, and told her what an idiot she was. At first I was just appalled, but then I realised that there were many times I hadn't behaved much better myself. I didn't swear at

Mum and I wasn't violent towards her or in front of her, but I did ignore her a lot, and I was often moody and selfish. Sometimes I was downright rude, just like that girl. It was like a wakeup call.

I turned the spotlight on myself that day, and as the girl went on and on behind me, I found myself thinking about the meaning and importance of grace. Susie Elelman had talked about grace in her modelling course, and when I thought about it I realised that the people I most admired in life were those that were graceful - not necessarily in terms of physical poise, but in terms of goodwill and generosity of spirit. I realised I was treating Mum like my servant and that I often acted like a brat. That last Christmas we'd gone shopping for presents and when she asked me what I wanted I wrote 'Nothing. No-one loves me anyway'. I might have been starting to look like a young woman but I was still behaving like a child. I knew I had to change my attitude.

It's a well know fact that like attracts like. Friendly, cheerful people attract the same. So from that day forwards I decided I was going to be more positive and more graceful. I was going to treat Mum like a human being and not a whipping post. I was going to behave like an adult. I didn't want to be driven by anger anymore, no matter what the reason. In a way, I had to feel grateful to that girl on the bus. She was like a mirror for me. It might have taken me a long time to realise it but it was time to grow up.

CHAPTER 14

Gender inequality is still a problem today but things were much worse in the 1970s. Despite the women's liberation movement the prevalent thinking of the time was still that of the 'little lady' and of 'good housekeeping'. Women in society were often treated as little more than grown up girls, and being a school dropout didn't put me in a good starting position. Add to that the way that disabilities were perceived and you'll get the picture - outside of marriage my opportunities were limited, to say the least.

Tom Dryden worked in the bank next door to Mum's milk bar and he sometimes came in to buy lollies when I was working there. He asked me out several times, but I was with Lindsay at the time, and I wasn't sure about Tom. He was pleasant enough, but there was something I couldn't put my finger on, something odd about him. Mum felt sorry for him and eventually suggested I go with him to see If I liked him. She said if I went out with him once he probably wouldn't bother me again anyway, so I might as well get it over with. Hah! Mothers are really good for their daughters' egos, aren't they? Anyway, now that my confidence was on the rise I thought I'd give it a go, so we arranged to watch 'The Rocky Horror Picture Show' together.

I shouldn't have listened to Mum. Tom was very intense. He can't have seen much of 'The Rocky Horror Picture Show' as he was too busy staring at me. And his shyness made me look like the most confident person in the world. He went to put his arm around me several times but always pulled back at the last minute. Eventually I got sick of it and pulled his arm around my shoulders myself. When Tom dropped me home after the movie I vowed never to go out with him again, but a few weeks later I found myself going to meet his family. I hadn't meant to, but he came over to my place and sat on the step for hours, until I finally relented.

Tom had a large family and they welcomed me warmly. I got on very well with his sisters and his little brother Roger, who was mesmerised by how I could talk to people without actually speaking. Roger was always hanging around and I think he may have had a crush on me. There were often family parties at Tom's place and in the end we stayed friends for many years. I hadn't been part of a large family since leaving England and the Drydens made me nostalgic for my childhood in Bolton.

Tom's father said I would be welcome at their home anytime. I think he hoped that Tom and I would marry one day. I heard him telling Tom to treat me well, because if he did he might be able to help me regain my voice. I know he only meant well, but there was the innuendo again; the reminder that I wasn't completely whole.

Despite the awkwardness Tom and I did have some good times together. We went to some Elvis Fan Club meetings and to a Cliff Richard concert. But when he told the neighbours that he had bought a rifle to shoot himself because I wouldn't marry him, I thought it best to call it quits.

After the milk bar closed I was out of a job. Back then it was shameful to be on welfare but I knew I was a burden on my parents. I didn't want to go on the 'dole' but I didn't seem to have much choice in the matter - when I went for an interview at the Department of Social Security I was told not to bother looking for work because I was disabled and as far as they were concerned I was 'unemployable'. I was told at the interview that I should get married and have children, because that was about the only role I was qualified for. In the meantime, the dole was my only option.

The whole process was humiliating. If you were on the dole in those days, you were thought of as a 'bludger', and even where we lived in the housing commission area work was a matter of pride. I had a friend who went so far as to tell people he was a sign writer for the government, rather than admit he was on unemployment benefits. But no one in their right mind was going to employ an unskilled girl who had dropped out of school and who couldn't even speak. What could I do?

Then, out of the blue, there was a knock on the front door. Two men in dark suits stood on the doorstep. The shorter one wore thick horn-rimmed glasses. He said they were caseworkers from the Department of Social Security, and that they had come to follow up on my recent interview. Mum made them a cup of tea and sat them down on the lounge. The taller man didn't say much - it felt like he was just staring at me the whole time. But the man with the glasses talked about a rehabilitation centre that had been set up at Mt Wilga to help people like me, people who needed help to integrate into society. He told me I would be given board and lodging at this centre and would also be given a stipend, a little extra money as a living allowance, while I learned applicable skills such as typing and bookkeeping.

The idea tempted me, I must admit, but there was something in the way the taller man looked at me that I didn't trust. Men in suits have always disconcerted me and it all sounded a little too good to be true. In any case, they arranged for me to visit the rehabilitation centre to see what it was like, and they were confident that I would want to stay. I was a bit apprehensive, but Mum was enthusiastic, so I agreed to go and have a look around.

It was a sunny day when we went to look around the complex, which was near Hornsby in the north of Sydney. I was shown around the classrooms, the dining and recreational areas, the medical room and the sleeping quarters. It all looked very nice and well kept but I still had a sense of foreboding. The women there didn't look very happy. None of them were laughing or playing around, and it all seemed a bit too 'controlled', almost like a prison.

I expressed these concerns when we finished the tour. The woman who was showing us around didn't seem surprised. "Of course some of them seem subdued," she said. "They're on medication." She looked at Mum. "It's necessary to keep order in a place like this," she said. "All the women are on the pill so their menstrual cycles will be regular.

They're given sleeping tablets at night and tranquilisers during the day." She leaned closer. "It helps make the transition from home to the outside world easier on them," she said.

I was shocked. I couldn't believe that they medicated their charges for no other reason than 'convenience'. When I heard this, the woman lost me. No way was I going to be doped up to make life easier. Not after my experience in the psych ward. I shook my head. I refused to join the program.

The two men in suits came back and things went downhill from there. I tried to explain that the rehabilitation centre was not the right place for me. I argued in painstaking paragraphs that it might be appropriate for people who needed physical help, like paraplegics or severe accident cases, but that there was nothing wrong with me. Nothing like that, anyway. I didn't need to be drugged or manipulated - all I needed was a few training courses that I could enrol for at the nearest technical college. The men in suits didn't agree. They threatened to cut my unemployment benefits if I didn't join the centre.

For several weeks I was terrified of what they would do. In my experience, government institutions were to be feared, rather than trusted. They had traumatised me at the psychiatric hospital, and I could see nothing to stop them from doing so again, especially if some public servant got a bee in his bonnet about me being uncooperative or something. I waited and waited for bad news, and then one day a letter came, asking me to go to the Commonwealth Employment Service office to see a man named Mike Morphett, who was in charge of 'special' cases.

On the day of the interview, I was kept waiting long beyond my appointment time. The day was hot, and even with the air conditioning whirring on the wall above, I was sweating and agitated. After a while I really wanted a cold drink, and the more I thought about it the thirstier I became. I was worried that Mr Morphett and I wouldn't get off to a good start. Not knowing what they were going to do next was making me feel paranoid.

By the time I was called in to Mr Morphett's office I was a bit of a mess, but in the end I needn't have worried - Mike was a genuinely compassionate man. He gave me a glass of water and waited patiently while I wrote it all down - my arguments against going to the rehabilitation centre and my fears of being medicated. After reading what I had written he flicked through the papers on his desk. He seemed puzzled. "Of course you don't want to go there," he frowned. "That place isn't for you." Then he smiled. "How about we enrol you in a typing course at the technical college instead?" I breathed a sigh of relief. It was just what I had asked for. Finally, I thought; someone who actually listens to me.

And so it was that I started my training to be a typist. Mr Morphett was true to his word and in fact went out of his way to help me. He told me about a trial scheme to train disabled people who wished to transition into the workplace. If I wanted to, I could be one of the first to try it, Mr Morphett told me, but it was very important that I finish the course because If I did well then the scheme would be implemented at a wider level, but if I dropped out then the government might not let any others take advantage of it.

Mr Morphett was the first government employee I met that treated me like a normal person, rather than something that should be swept under the carpet. He made me feel that I was a regular job hunter, just looking for work like everyone else. He was very down to earth and didn't dally about with platitudes or false sympathy. "You have to look forwards, not backwards," he told me.

Mr Morphett left the Commonwealth Employment Service before I graduated from my studies, so I never had an opportunity to properly thank him for helping me, or to tell him how far I had come since first meeting him that day. I heard, years later, that he had left the CES because he couldn't help people as much as he wanted to; he had been restricted in how much he could do. Well, all I can say is that if he hadn't helped me at that particular time in my life, I don't know how things might have turned out. Would there have been another Mr Morphett to put me on the right path? Who knows?

After some preparation, Mr Morphett arranged for me to take a receptionist course at Williams Business College in Wollongong. The course included bookkeeping, typing and shorthand. I was wary at first, but Mr Morphett wouldn't let me come up with any excuses to avoid attending. He made sure I received payments for any books I needed and he even fronted up for my bus fares for the first week, with money from his own pocket.

The hardest thing about being back in a classroom was learning to overcome the conditioning that was a result of my time at St Anne's. I had to put aside my embarrassment at having to write every question down on paper and I had to learn to relate to my teachers. At first I was nervous, waiting for the bad stuff to start. I expected yelling and name calling, and ultimately I imagined that the course would end with me running back home for safety. But I didn't want to fail after all Mr Morphett had done for me, and after a couple of weeks I realised that the teachers at Williams Business College weren't my enemies and weren't out to get me as Father Moran or Sisters Kathryn and St Patrick had been. And once I began to relax and let it all soak in I found that I actually enjoyed studying a lot more than I expected.

Outside the classroom was as much a learning curve for me as inside but I was determined to succeed. Buying lunch was somewhere between amusing and nerve wracking the first few times, but I had learned a few tricks at Mum's milk bar and soon I didn't need my notepad anymore - I just pointed to whatever I wanted on my sandwiches. Meanwhile, I made a few new friends at WBC. I was especially close with the two other girls who were on the 'trial' scheme with me. Both of them had spinal injuries. I can't remember their names now, but we were good friends at the time, and I remember realising that their situations were much harder than mine.

I finished up at Williams Business College with a certificate for completing the receptionist course that Mr Morphett had nominated me for, and an additional certificate in secretarial skills. It turned out that I was a good student after all, and I managed to achieve more in the six months than was planned. On top of the other certifications, I was awarded a certificate in telephony, even though I couldn't speak. How did I manage that, you might ask? Well, believe it or not, the exam was written, rather than verbal. Throughout the years that followed it always tickled me that I was certified to answer a telephone, despite being voiceless.

The CES scheme was set up so that I continued to receive government payments while I attended the courses at Williams Business College. With my first payment I bought a beige gabardine raincoat from Badrans, across the road. Badrans was a modern shop with expensive clothes that I would never have thought of buying before. But with Susie Elelman's training still in mind I decided that it was important to dress the part, and what's more, I was pretty sure it made me look like a movie star.

Chapter 15

When I was seventeen I spent many Saturday nights with Mum and Dad at the Shellharbour Workers' Club. As I wasn't yet old enough to go out by myself, I would sit with them in the lounge while they played darts with their friends. I was proud of Dad, who was the NSW darts champion for several years, but I was more interested in the music filtering down from the auditorium upstairs; I wanted to go dancing.

Dad had been a regular at the Workers' Club since we'd settled in Shellharbour. Being such a good darts player, he was urged to join the competition team that played there every Tuesday night, and soon enough there were trophies all around the house. Whenever there was a social game of darts everyone wanted to be paired with Dad because they knew he would probably win. That's how he met most of his new friends, including his best mate Cliff. Dad made a lasting pact with Cliff to split the winnings if either of them ever won any prize money.

Our 'extended family' came into being after Mum's sister Mary died. Nana had returned to the UK and Mum was feeling down. Dad asked Cliff if he and his wife Marge would come over on Christmas Eve to help cheer her up.

Mum bought a few longnecks of beer for Dad and Cliff and a bottle of sherry to share with Marge. She figured a dozen sausage rolls and some nibbles would do for a snack and that evening I helped her set everything out nicely, ready for our visitors. What we didn't know was that word had spread and that the entire darts team and their families were about to turn up for the party.

When the doorbell kept ringing Mum began to freak out. She and Dad were brought up to always provide for guests, so it stung her pride to realise we didn't have enough food and drink for everybody. "What are we going to do, Marie?" she asked, with a note of panic in her voice. Well, as it happened the Aussie custom of 'bringing a plate' worked its spell. Everyone who turned up that night brought food and drink to share, and in the end we even had leftovers. Everyone had a great time and Mum was well and truly cheered up. I think she understood the tradition of bringing a plate a little better after that night. She saw how it helped neighbours and friends get together to enjoy each other's company without anyone being burdened.

Each Christmas Eve from that year forwards, the darts team and their families would turn up at our place to make a night of it. The men would sit outside drinking beer and racing Christmas beetles, and now and then you would hear a loud moan that sounded like a wounded cow, which was actually them singing along with the Carols by Candlelight broadcast. The women sat inside, talking about anything and everything, and occasionally drowning out the men with their more melodious voices. Most of the team were immigrants like us, so not many had extended families around. A few, like Cliff, were Aussies, but they always came along anyway. Dad said their real families could wait because our 'extended family' was better.

It was at the annual darts dinner at the Shellharbour Workers' Club that I met Darren, the son of one of Dad's mates. I went out with Darren for a few months but most of our 'dates' were with our parents. Darren was an avid darts player but he didn't like dancing, so he didn't want to go upstairs to the auditorium, and he didn't like going to the movies either. I should have realised that we weren't really compatible, but I was still pretty naïve. I thought our parents were the problem and that we'd have fun once they were out of the picture. I imagined that things would get romantic when we were alone together, but the truth was that Darren didn't have a romantic bone in his body - he just liked playing darts and drinking with his mates.

Darren and I were engaged on my eighteenth birthday. He insisted that I had made a good catch in him, because I was disabled. "Who else would want to marry you?" he asked.

Before we were engaged Darren used to come around to my place every weekend, but afterwards he stopped making the effort. He seemed to think that I would find my fill in life just staying over at his house, looking after him. But the more I got to know what he was really like, the less I fancied him. I found out why we always went out with his parents - they paid for everything. I found out that the 'tomato plants' in his backyard were not actually tomato plants. I found out that he didn't even buy the engagement ring he gave me - his mother did. It got worse and worse. The bruise around his mother's eye - he did it. The reason he hammered his dog to death - because One-Eighty barked and tried to defend me when he raised his fists against me. I ran out in tears that day, but Darren didn't even deal with One-Eighty's dinner bowl - it was seething with maggots the next time I went over.

I probably shouldn't have even gone back, but I didn't know any better. That night I went to bed while Darren and his mates stayed up doing whatever they did. I was feeling depressed about the relationship and before I knew it I had fallen into one of my drowning nightmares. This one was particularly vivid - I had been swept into a sewer and couldn't claw my way out. I even heard laughter as I struggled to stay above the surface, as though someone thought it was funny.

I coughed and spluttered my way back to reality but I still felt clammy when I opened my eyes. I wasn't sure what was happening but the light was on and I could hear laughter and voices. My pj's and blanket smelled bad. I sat up in horror as I worked out what was going on. Darren had urinated on me while I was asleep. It was only then that I made sense of what he was saying. "I can do anything I want to her," he leered. "She can't scream and she won't leave me." I stared at him in shock. He had come into the bedroom with two of his friends. "You guys have a go," he said to his mates. "Go on!"

I didn't tell my parents what Darren had done to me but I made it clear that it was over. Mum and Dad still saw him at the club from time to time and they said he always asked about me. But I wasn't interested in seeing him again. The way he treated me was an atrocious experience that didn't need to be revisited.

One of Elvis Presley's last hits during his lifetime was a cover of the song 'Hurt'. Elvis' life had been messy since splitting with Priscilla, and he had already put himself into a coma after overdosing on barbiturates a few years earlier. But things had gotten worse since then, and on 16 August 1977 the unthinkable finally happened - Elvis left the building for ever. At first I didn't believe he had died, but a couple of days later the newspapers reported his funeral. It was heartbreaking. They said that eighty thousand fans had lined the processional route from Graceland to the Forest Hill Cemetery where he was buried. Later on I learned that his physician, Dr Nichopoulos, had prescribed him more than ten thousand doses of sedatives, amphetamines and narcotics that year alone. If you watch clips from his last concerts you can see how out of it he was - laughing and crying his way through his performances as though he barely knew where he was.

I was looking for a job when I heard that Elvis had died. I had successfully graduated from Williams Business College but it still wasn't as easy as all that. People made up the craziest excuses to avoid employing me. The recruiter at Woolworths thought that I wouldn't be able to hear the fire alarm if it went off. One business said I was too young, another that I was too old. David Jones, the department store, said they'd let me know when they started employing office assistants again but they must have really long-lived staff there as I still haven't heard from them, forty years later.

So much for gainful employment! Without a job I had a lot of time on my hands. I wasn't going to the Spiritualist Church regularly anymore but I'd still attend a service now and then, when I felt like it. One Sunday, Mark started giving me a hard time about 'letting go' of what had happened at school as it was 'holding me back' and making me unhappy. He wasn't wrong about St Anne's but he didn't have the whole picture. He didn't know about Darren. He didn't understand the impact that Elvis' death was having on me. And little did he know that I had recently met Chris, who was into even more interesting things than spiritualism. Chris belonged to a coven, and claimed he was a warlock.

Chris used to meet up with me on the beach at Warilla, where we would spend several hours walking around or just sitting on the sand while he told me about the world he lived in. Soon enough I went to a coven meeting with him and was surprised by how ordinary it was. Coven meetings were usually held at a member's home, just like with Christian groups. At that first meeting they talked about 'celebrations' for Halloween, or 'All Hallows Eve', as they called it. I didn't understand everything that they said, but I got the impression that I hadn't been with them long enough to take part in the celebrations. "You can come another time," Chris told me, "when they are more sure of you, and you make the commitment, like I know you will."

By 1978 Courtney was engaged to her long-term boyfriend, Paul, who was in the navy. Courtney was still living in Dapto but they would come and pick me up on the weekends and we would do 'stuff'. Most often this just meant driving around Wollongong, up and down Marine Drive and Crown Street, listening to the radio.

On hot summer nights we would stop for ice creams and wander around the Wollongong lighthouse. The movie 'Grease' was a huge hit that year, and "You're the One that I Want" by Olivia Newton-John and John Travolta was always playing. Courtney and I also loved Olivia's song 'Hopelessly Devoted to You'.

'Grease' was the word and was also the reason I met Robert, Paul's navy mate, who was stationed at HMAS Albatross at Nowra. Courtney arranged a double date and I especially remember the night we went to see 'Grease' because Robert bought me a box of Maltesers and I accidently left them on the floor of the cinema, under my seat. I knew I must like Robert because ordinarily I would never forget chocolate!

I would have liked to have carried on seeing Robert but 'duty called' and soon he was moved to another naval base, and we drifted apart. Three or four years later I bumped into him again at the Windang Bowling Club. He scared the life out of me when he grabbed me from behind while I was dancing. I still liked him but it wasn't to be - his new girlfriend was already throwing daggers at me with her eyes.

Around this time I finally found a part time job at the newly opened Warilla Advice and Information Service (now known as the Warilla Neighbourhood Centre). The building was situated on Shellharbour Road, about half an hour's walk from my place, and I'd be there every Monday, without fail. I started out helping around the office, but soon I was doing whatever needed doing, apart from answering the telephone, of course. After all my training at WBC I took to it like a duck to water. It was a relief to be *doing* something at last.

One my regular tasks was to type up correspondence for people in the local community. I remember typing dozens of letters for an elderly gentleman who wanted to change the world. He came in every week with a complaint against one government department or another, and he always gave me a Kit Kat after I'd finished helping him. I thought he was funny and his letters were interesting and made some good points about government legislation. I don't know if anything ever came of them but there were so many we could have compiled a book.

During my time at the centre I also centralised their filing system. I organised everything into filing cabinets, cross-referenced with index cards so that information could be easily found. The Women's Rape Centre shared our rooms, so I typed some reports for them as well. Seeing all those women who had been abused and pushed aside made me feel a little more resolved about myself and what I had been through. I wasn't completely alone, I realised - others had suffered more than me.

For a while I wondered if I would be able to talk about my personal troubles with the counsellor who worked at the centre. She seemed really nice and she was very patient when communicating with me, but ultimately I couldn't do it. In a way she was my boss, and it didn't feel right. Also, in those days I thought it was my own cross to bear. Like Nana used to advise me, I just got on with it – life, that is.

Meanwhile, every Friday, come rain or shine, I would walk down to the Commonwealth Employment Service on George Street, and I would go through every available job on the vacancies board. Mr Morphett had moved on but I used to see the same staff lady each week and we would usually have a coffee together, because I'd be there for several hours. She would call up every job on the board on my behalf and we played a game to break up the monotony of rejection - we would try to guess which excuse each employer would come up with to avoid interviewing me for the job.

In reality I could have forced any one of those companies to employ me, because none of their excuses were valid. But the truth is that I didn't want to work for someone who didn't want to employ me. I wanted work to be enjoyable and something I could throw myself into, and I needed an employer who recognised my skills and wanted me around. Fortunately, my 'careers advisor', as I had come to call her, agreed, and together we searched the whole Wollongong area for an employer who would appreciate a loyal worker and who wasn't so narrow minded.

Alas, despite our best efforts, Wollongong didn't want me. In the end my big break came in Sydney, and as usual it came from an unexpected source.

I had sat the Australian Public Service test with about fifty other people just after finishing at Williams Business College, but I had forgotten all about it in the months since then, so it was quite a surprise when I received a letter asking me to attend an interview for a job with the Department of Social Security in Sydney. My first thought was NO. I didn't really trust the government, and I didn't want to work for them. On top of not wanting to work for the DSS I remember being very apprehensive about catching the train and finding my way around Sydney by myself.

I took the letter along to the Commonwealth Employment Service to show my 'careers advisor' but while I was explaining to her that I didn't want to work at the DSS, Mr Burke, the new CES Manager, came over. Mr Burke was a smooth operator. He explained that I could work for any government department, not just the DSS. He said they weren't all bad, and that I should keep an open mind. The speech he gave me was pretty convincing. Not all of my experiences with the government had been negative, he made me realise. What about Mr Morphett and the other staff at the CES who had helped me? What about Helen, my first social worker? She worked for the government too. It stood to reason that there must be lots of good people working in government jobs. After a while Mr Burke suggested that I give it a try. If I didn't like it after one month then he would personally place me back on unemployment benefits himself.

I tried the excuse of not having enough money to get to Sydney but Mr Burke got out his wallet and gave me ten dollars. "There," he said. "That should take care of the train fare and your lunch." What could I do? I was outwitted. But I was still worried. This wasn't long after the Granville railway disaster. 83 people had died and more than 200 were injured when a locomotive derailed and caused a bridge to collapse onto the passenger carriages. I knew the chances of such accidents were very low but I still half expected something similar to happen to me on the trip up to Sydney. Even when the journey itself went fine I found all those tall city buildings overwhelming, and then having to go up, oh my God, twenty floors or more in a rickety lift to reach the interview room - it's a wonder I didn't lose my breakfast.

My interview at the Department of Social Security HQ in Sydney was on a Thursday. Despite my apprehension I must have made a reasonable impression, because I was immediately offered a job in the typing pool, starting the following Monday. I had one day and the weekend to get myself organised. I was about to start a new life!

Chapter 16

It was still dark outside when I left the house that Monday morning, but I had to catch the six o'clock train at Wollongong station if I was to get to Sydney in time to clock on at eight thirty. I couldn't stop yawning but I was thrilled - it was my first day of real work; work that I would get paid for. I was a typist for the Department of Social Security and I was going to live in Sydney! I was about to start a new chapter of my life.

I sat on the train with the little suitcase that I'd bought on the weekend. I hadn't had much time to prepare, but I had two new skirts and tops and a summer jacket from Katies to get me started. I felt proud to be buying clothes for work, just like any other normal person. When I told Mum and Dad that I'd been offered the job in Sydney, they were over the moon too, but Mum did the usual mother thing; the nay saying. "You can't go to Sydney on your own," she fretted. "What will become of you?"

Mum finally relented, but not before buying me a silver whistle from the jewellers. It came with a chain so that I could wear it around my neck and blow it if I ever needed help. She was just looking out for me, like any mother would, but I thought she was being silly. What would I need help for? I was nineteen years old and gainfully employed. I could look after myself.

The train to Sydney had those old wooden carriages with hard leather seats and caged heaters at each end. Most of the passengers who got on with me were workmen, heading to the mines at Coledale. They looked permanently tired with their smudged black eyes and their grubby overalls. No one spoke much, and most of them snoozed during the journey. I don't know how they didn't miss their stop, but somehow they woke up just as the train pulled in at their station. Then they stretched and dragged themselves out into the cold morning.

The sky gradually lightened up as the train chugged up the hill through the Royal National Park. Station by station more people got on, and by the time we reached Sutherland the carriage was already full of office workers… like me.

I had a moment of anxiety when I arrived at Sydney's Central station without really knowing where to go. But then I remembered that I had to change from the country platforms to the City Circle line, so I followed the crowds and was relieved to find it wasn't too difficult. A few minutes later I found myself walking between Wynyard and the DSS headquarters, just up from Martin Place. I can still smell the air of the city on that day - a hint of petrol mixed with… what was it? Smoke? Dust? The shops were just opening and everybody was rushing on their way to work. For the first time in my life I felt like a real grown up. I stopped at a fruit cart and thought of Nana's father Charlie, my great grandfather, who had been a barrow boy. I bought an apple and the man put an extra one in the bag for me, for free.

Pat Shannon was the typing supervisor at the DSS HQ. I left my suitcase in her office and was herded into a room with the other new employees for an induction meeting. We filled out all the necessary forms and were told how things worked in the public service. We were then formed into groups of four, and my group was taken taken to Clarence Street, where I was assigned to work as a typist at the office of the Commonwealth Rehabilitation Service. When I realised who I was working for my heart nearly stopped. It was the CRS that managed the Mt Wilga rehabilitation centre that the Social Security suits had tried to make me go to, a couple of years earlier. I took a deep breath and hoped they wouldn't remember me.

As it turned out I needn't have worried. The CRS was a very big office with different cells that dealt with different areas of rehabilitation - Mt Wilga was only one of their operations, and no one had any idea of my former brush with that place. My fears allayed, I took in my new workplace. The typing pool was a lot nicer than I expected. The room was open plan with big windows that looked out onto the city and the harbour. There were only eight girls in the pool, including Barbara, our supervisor.

We each had our own desk with a new electric typewriter. This was the first time I used an electric typewriter, and I thought it was a wonderful invention. It even had an auto correct button - there'd be no more messy liquid paper. The work wasn't too demanding and we stopped twice a day for tea breaks. One of the girls explained that it was union rules - we had to take a break for twenty minutes every morning and afternoon. I didn't know much about unions but I was impressed. All in all I was very happy with my new job.

As my first day at work ended I had a visit from the staff social worker, who wanted to make sure I found somewhere to stay. I was planning to check in at the YWCA if I couldn't find anything else, but he said he knew of a new hostel in Kirribilli that was opening, so we went for a drive over the bridge to check it out.

The Kirribilli hostel was still being renovated but it had windows that looked out over the water. Luna Park was just a stone's throw away, although it wasn't yet infamous; this was still a few months before six children lost their lives in the tragic Ghost Train fire. There were no locks on any of the hostel doors and the bathrooms were shared, but it had been a long day so I decided to stay the night and look for somewhere else tomorrow.

The next morning I opened my window and stretched, breathing in the fresh air. 'Here I am Sydney, come and get me,' I said in my head, feigning a confidence I didn't really have. The water glimmered in the sunshine, and the smell of frangipanis floated through the window.

I made myself a quick coffee and grabbed my bag. On the way to work I memorised several landmarks so I would be able to find my way back that evening without getting lost. But I shouldn't have bothered, because that afternoon the social worker came to see me again, wanting to introduce me to a woman who could help me find a 'proper' home. As he took me to meet this woman, the social worker told me how much he loved Sydney; there was no better city in the world, he said. He was so enthusiastic, I wondered if all Sydneysiders were like him. I felt lucky to work for an organisation that took such good care of its employees.

The woman the social worker introduced me to belonged to an organisation that were funded to relocate out-of-towners, like me. She told me about a house on Darlinghurst Road that was owned by the Returned and Services League. It was several storeys high, and she said they rented out 'bedsitter' rooms.

I went to look at the RSL house in Kings Cross straight away. It wasn't fancy but the rooms were just $50 per week, including linen and breakfast. The building was a bit musty but it had character, with high ceilings and a mosaic flooring that made click-click noises as I walked around. I was shown a small self-contained room with French doors that opened out onto a balcony. I thought it was very chic. There was a shared bathroom and a lounge room with a TV on each floor of the house, and there was an urn of hot water on each floor as well, so I could go and make coffee, tea or my go-to dinner of cup-a-soup and crackers. Before I knew it I had traded up my lockless room in the Kirribilli hostel and moved in.

Most of the residents of the RSL house were retirees or people without homes of their own. One of the men on my floor was a Vietnam veteran; he was a permanent resident and had already been living there for a while. There were also two elderly ladies who I always met in the TV room. They were both widowed and without families, and they would go to bed at 8.30pm every night. After that I had the TV all to myself.

As the new Eastern Suburbs train service hadn't yet launched I started out taking the bus to work and back, but after the driver missed my stop a few times I took to walking. It was a 45 minute journey each way, but I was happy to be exercising and I loved my newfound independence. I also got to meet some of the local characters this way. The people around Kings

Cross in those days were a bit 'different'. It was hard to put my finger on it, but many of them seemed to be in a world of their own.

Mum was worried about me walking home at night time around 'that area', as she called it, but at the time I wasn't sure what she was talking about. Sure there were some eccentrics around, but I never felt unsafe and I didn't dally in any case. Some nights my mouth would water with the smell of fish and chips or hamburgers cooking in the takeaway joints around the Cross, but I always went home to my soup and crackers. I lived a simple lifestyle: a 'chat' with the old ladies (me with my trusty notebook and pen) and then TV or a paperback until bedtime. Then, in the morning, I would get up at 6am and dash to the bathroom before anyone else got in there before me.

Work continued to go well. The CRS was a remarkably stress-free environment and I became friends with many of the girls in my typing pool, especially Veronica, who was always asking me to go out dancing with her. I wanted to join her but I was nervous at first; Mum's words of warning still rang in my ears and despite my newly found independence I was concerned that I wouldn't really be able to look after myself if something went wrong. Sure, I had my whistle, but what would happen if I got lost somewhere in the city and I couldn't use a payphone to call a taxi? Or something worse?

Veronica was an Aboriginal woman. Her skin was beautifully black and she didn't have to cheat to get a fashionable afro; hers was natural. She was as skinny as a supermodel and as a dancer she would have given Michael Jackson a run for his money - she had all his moves down to a tee. When I eventually got up the courage to go out with her I had nothing but fun. She was so good that whenever she got up to dance everyone would form a circle around her; they would 'give her the floor'.

Before too long I was going out with Veronica every weekend and I was hooked on disco. I loved the whole scene, and it was liberating to be able to dance the night away without anyone asking me why I couldn't speak. Dancing was a language of its own and the music was too loud to really hear anyone anyway. One time we went to a disco that was run by Donnie Sutherland, the TV personality. There were a few famous faces there but it wasn't that great; there were too many 'barbie dolls' vying for attention.

Me and Veronica preferred regular discos, where we had more fun. Veronica's favourite place was near where she lived in Manly. Sometimes we would dance there all night and then I'd 'crash' at her apartment before catching a ferry back in the morning.

Veronica knew I didn't eat properly at the RSL house so she would sometimes take me to cafés and restaurants where we could get a proper meal at lunchtime. The canteen at work served three options but they were all pretty ordinary. Veronica liked a vegetarian place around the corner from our office. I didn't think much of the savoury food there, but they had an apple pie to die for.

After a while Veronica suggested that we find a flat to share because we got on so well. I remember her telling me that she might as well put the government cheques she got to good use. She was talking about the allowance that she received from Aboriginal Affairs each fortnight. She'd told them that she didn't want the allowance but they kept giving it to her anyway. Veronica said she didn't want any handouts and didn't like being thought of as a 'welfare case'. She was like every other Australian, she said. Just like me she had left home to find work in the city, and as we were on the same wage she didn't see why she should get any extra benefits. Veronica said her mum had a lot of kids to feed, so I suggested that she send her the cheques. "That won't work," she said. When I asked why not she just shook her head and changed the subject, so I let it go, even though I didn't really understand her logic.

Veronica was a great friend, but we never did get the flat together because she went missing soon afterwards. One Monday she just didn't turn up for work. Knowing her to be a bit of a wild card I didn't think anything of it until two detectives came to question us at the typing pool, later that week. I was known as her best friend so I was questioned longest. But I couldn't help. I hadn't seen her since the previous Friday as I'd gone home to see my parents in Warilla that weekend.

Apparently, Veronica had been seen on the Monday morning at the local pie shop, where she always got her breakfast. The pie shop was just across the road from our office but for some reason she didn't make it over - she literally just disappeared. The police questioned her most recent boyfriend, thinking that they might have had a fight, but he didn't know anything, and neither did her other friends. The question came up about her maybe going 'walkabout' but this was my Veronica they were talking about. She was a city girl. She liked work and she loved going out clubbing. She wouldn't just go walkabout, would she?

When the detectives talked to me they wanted to know if I had noticed anyone paying her more attention than usual. They asked if there had been any strange men hanging around at the discos? If I hadn't been so sad I would have laughed. Of course there were plenty of strange men hanging around at discos. There always were!

One of the policemen said that Aboriginal Australians had been 'taken' before, for the sex slave trade. I had heard of sex slaves but for some reason I had always pictured them as skinny blonde girls. Well, Veronica was skinny - that was true. The policeman said that pure blood black girls were sometimes targeted too.

I waited and waited for Veronica to come back and I stopped going out to discos - it wasn't the same without her. But days, weeks and then months went by without news. Every time I went to head office I would ask if anyone had heard from her but the answer was always no. When Veronica's flat was eventually cleaned out the welfare cheques were still in the drawer where she had left them, never cashed.

CHAPTER 17

A few months after my friend Veronica disappeared there was a major train strike. I was visiting my family in Warilla at the time so Mum called Pat Shannon, the typing supervisor at Sydney HQ, as I stood by. I'd stuck to my resolution to go easier on Mum and it was paying off - I was no longer taking her for granted, and now, after everything we had been through, we were finally becoming close again. Pat asked if I would be willing to work at the Wollongong office of the DSS while the strike lasted. I was worried I might lose my job so I nodded without hesitation. "Of course she'd be happy with that," Mum said. "She could even manage the tea trolley if you want her to." I narrowed my eyes but couldn't help smiling as Mum grinned cheekily at me. Pat said she would see what she could arrange.

So it happened that I was transferred to the Wollongong DSS. There were ten of us in the typing pool but our office was a step down from the Clarence Street set-up in Sydney. There was enough room to move around, but the space was cramped and there were no big windows with city views as there had been at the CRS. Here we had small windows that looked out onto the car park in front of the building. The windows were double glazed with venetian blinds between the panes of glass. The blinds were usually half closed to keep out the sun, but at the same time this made the interior of our office seem a bit gloomy.

I started work in Wollongong every morning at 8am on the nose, and the workday was pretty regimented: we had tea breaks at 11am and 3pm, lunch was at 12.30pm, and then I was off home at 5pm every afternoon. Talking wasn't tolerated while we worked, unless it was work- related. The girls still managed to chat now and then, but only for short periods of time. The rest of the time we just typed.

Typing for eight hours a day might sound like a fate worse than death, but I actually loved it. For one thing, I learnt how to make forms and charts on the typewriter during this time. It was really an art form back then, as everything had to be done manually; I even measured the tab stop with a ruler, so that everything would be exactly aligned. It might sound menial but from my perspective I had found something I could excel at.

Every day we were given a pile of letters to type, and we then had to take each finished letter back to the clerk whom they 'belonged' to. I hadn't had much contact with the clerical staff up in Sydney so these interactions were unusual for me. They made life a bit more social, and even if I only got an "Oh, hi Marie," it was still more conversation than I was used to.

Seamus was a clerk that I noticed straight away. He was one of those tall, good looking guys that should have been a model, and he knew it. He would come into the typing pool and sit on my desk, casual as can be, leaning over towards me to discuss what he needed.

The clatter of the typewriters would slow down as the girls in the pool eyed him up and down. The movie 'American Gigolo' was on at the cinemas and Seamus was a dead ringer for the young Richard Gere. This coincidence helped him get what he wanted when he wanted it, and I was no exception. Seamus was so charming that I just couldn't say no when he asked if I would urgently type a report up for him. I really should have made him wait in turn, but what the hell, one look from those deep brown eyes and I was there.

Part of Seamus's job was to go out and interview clients in their homes. As a field officer, his role was to get information that the department needed, but he also had to decide if he thought there was any funny business going on. If the client was a single mother, for instance, Seamus would look to see how many wine glasses were at the sink, or whether there were any men's shoes under the bed or lounge. He was kind of like a private eye for the government.

So these were the reports that Seamus would bring me to type, these 'home visits'. It was very interesting work, to be honest. Not only did I type the background notes but I also typed up what was called an 'I said, he said' document, where client conversations would be written just as they were spoken. I didn't mind doing Seamus's reports for him, as they were a bit like chapters in a spy novel. A spy novel by a very handsome government agent.

Seamus aside, I sorted my files out each day so that I could start with the shortest letters and end on the longest. I liked to get the little stuff out of the way, and then concentrate on the harder tasks later on. I would make it a point to always finish my work and sometimes I would volunteer for extra assignments too.

As if I wasn't working hard enough already, Lee, my new supervisor, sometimes delegated her own work to me when she was busy. Back then I was convinced that she didn't like me, as she always seemed to give her work to me, rather than anyone else. But when I bumped into her, years later, I found out how wrong I had been. Lee explained that she hadn't singled me out for any negative reason; she'd only given me the work because she knew that I would do it, and do it well. She said that she had always respected me, and that I was the best team member she'd had in those days.

Around the time, however, one of the other typists complained about me, telling Lee that I didn't do my work 'properly'. She argued that this was why I completed everything so quickly, because I wasn't doing a good job. Much to my surprise, Lee jumped to my defence. She said that the real reason I got through more work than the others was because I couldn't talk and didn't get caught up in their useless chatter. That was funny. For once my 'disability' was in my favour.

***

Work culture was very different at the end of the 1970s. We never called anyone by their first names, for a start; our superiors were always Mr or

Mrs This or Miss That. Also, us women never wore pants to work; we always wore dresses or skirts, which could be awkward when we had to climb those tall ladders in the file room. Some of the guys would inevitably be 'hanging around' when we were hoisting up our skirts to get up the ladders. They were gentleman, though, right? They weren't hanging around for anything other than to chivalrously help us down again. Mmm hmmm...

Travelling to the DSS office in Wollongong was a breeze compared to Sydney. It still took me an hour on the bus, but it was so much easier than getting around in the big city. If I left home at 7am I'd arrive in Wollongong just before 8am. Then there was a quick dash up Crown Street to Market Street and voila, I was there.

Most of the drivers with the local bus company were good-natured. If I was running late they would sometimes pull in at the bottom of my street to pick me up. And as they got to know me they'd often have my ticket printed and ready for me when I came aboard. My mornings didn't differ much, but now and then this became a problem if I wanted to go somewhere different after work. For example, I occasionally met Mum at Warrawong to go department shopping at David Jones. Warrawong is halfway to Warilla from Wollongong, but if the driver had already printed out my ticket I used to just take it and wear the extra expense. I didn't want to upset them by trying to explain that I was getting off the bus earlier than usual.

But there's always one, I guess, and it was no different with John J Hill's buses; one of the newer drivers didn't share the generous spirit of his colleagues. It made no difference if I stood up and pulled the cord for my stop, near Benaud Crescent, or if waited near the front of the bus next to him. Either way he refused to stop for me. He once very loudly said that if I couldn't speak English I should damn well learn - he would stop for me when I could tell him where I wanted to get off. What could I do? It wasn't worth creating a scene over so I learned to pick my battles. If that particular driver didn't pull over at my stop I would just get off at the next one, near the Warilla Police Station.

This strategy actually ended up killing two birds with one stone, as it meant I could avoid Mrs Spratt, who lived a few doors down from us. Mrs Spratt called me names whenever I walked past her place on my way home. She still called me 'Dumbo' and she kept asking who had I slept with to get the DSS job. When the belligerent bus driver 'missed' my stop, I realised that I could avoid Mrs Spratt by walking down Benaud Crescent from the Warilla Police Station, instead of heading up the hill from my usual stop.

One day the bus broke down near the steelworks on the way home, and we all had to get off and wait for a replacement. Luckily it was one of the nice drivers that afternoon, and he sat on the grass with me while we waited. After we'd had a good 'chat' I realised how much my confidence had grown - I had held a pretty decent conversation with a stranger, without using my writing pad. The secret was that he helped me to expand on my answers by asking specific questions and paying attention to my body language and my hands as I 'talked'.

After the train strike ended I was kept on as a typist at the Wollongong DSS. The department was about to open a new office in Warilla, close to home, and Pat Shannon suggested that I transfer there, rather than coming back to Sydney. I would have preferred to stay in the Wollongong office now that I had made some new friends, but I didn't think much of it at the time - I was happy to just follow orders.

On what was meant to be my last day in the Wollongong office the other girls in the typing pool kept staring at me and no one sat with me at morning tea time. I didn't know what I had done wrong. Then Lee, our supervisor, approached me. "Marie, the girls think you are trying to take Casey's position away from her," she said. Casey was a new girl who started in the typing pool in Wollongong after me. She also lived near Warilla and wanted to work in the new office when it opened.

For some reason the girls had been told that I was stealing Casey's position at Warilla because I *didn't* want to stay in Wollongong. Someone was clearly lying about me. Later that day, the regional manager, Mr Whitehead, called me into his office. Authority figures still intimidated me, and it took all I had to hold myself together, but Mr Whitehead explained everything. It turned out that it was Casey herself who had spread the rumour - she had become very 'friendly' with one of the managers who was transferring to the Warilla office, and neither of them was pleased when I was offered the new typist's position there - I had gotten in the way of their plans to spend more time together.

Mr Whitehead said he would try to sort things out, but the damage had already been done, and back in the typing pool things rapidly went from bad to worse. "You only got the job in the first place because you're disabled," one of the women said. That really stung. I'd sat the public service test just like everyone else, and I had already proven myself as a diligent and capable employee in the Wollongong office *and* up in Sydney.

It upset me to have anyone think that I'd only been placed in the job because I was a 'charity case'. I felt that I had to work this out, to see if it was true, so I booked an appointment with the personnel manager at HQ and on my next flexi-day I took the train up to Sydney. I would have liked to have caught up with some of my friends from the CRS but I didn't even tell them I was coming - I was strictly on a mission to find out what was in my file.

After all that build-up, of course, it was anticlimactic when I finally sat down with the personnel officer and read the documents themselves. There was no mention whatsoever about any special treatment. My dossier simply contained my application, my test results, and my medical results, just like everyone else. I asked Pat Shannon about the accusation from my workmate, and she laughed it off. I think the word she used was 'bullshit'.

Even though the typing pool was separated from the rest of the DSS office in Wollongong, I had made friends with Seamus and some of the other clerical staff during my interactions with them. John Scott was a clerical officer and also the union rep, and I would sometimes have an apple cider with him and a few other mates at the Hotel Illawarra after work. When he heard about what had happened with the Warilla office, John started fuming. "Casey can't do that," he said. "What a bitch, making up stories just to keep you from going to work." I told him not to worry as I was happy to stay on in Wollongong anyway, but he wasn't having any of it. "That's not the point," he said. "You can't let yourself be walked over like that!"

The woman who claimed I'd received special treatment for being disabled had voiced the opinion that I shouldn't have the job as I couldn't answer the phone. Answering the phone was the only job I couldn't manage (despite my certificate from Williams Business College), but phone calls weren't listed in our statement of duties in any case. As typists we typed. Nothing else, just typed. But John thought he would fix things anyway. And he did.

The following Monday I was at my desk when Lee's phone rang. She picked it up and looked quizzically at me. Then she motioned for me to come over. "I know this sounds silly," she said, "but John Scott's on the phone, and he wants to talk to you." I just looked at her; I didn't know what to do. Lee got a bit cranky. "Oh, for God's sake Marie, just take the phone," she said. So I took the receiver from her and held it to my ear (upside down at first, to the amusement of the other girls who were all watching). I heard John's voice. "Don't panic, Marie," he said. "Just do as I say."

John told me to try scratching twice on the receiver for yes, and once for no. Then he asked me for a file. "Go and look for it on your desk," he said. "Come back and tap on the phone so I know you're there, and then tell me if you have it. With a dozen pairs of eyes on me I found the file and returned to Lee's desk. I tapped on the phone. "Have you got it?" John asked. I scratched twice for yes. "Fine, I'll be up in a minute to collect it," he said. "Now put the phone down and go back to your desk."

A moment later John came barrelling through the door that separated our office spaces. He headed straight over to my desk and I gave the file to him. Of course everybody was watching us, and he took the file with a flourish. "See, that's all it takes," he said, to no-one in particular. "Marie can answer the phone just fine. She's every bit as good as you lot."

You could hear a pin drop as John swept out the door again, and I couldn't help a little smile from turning up the corners of my mouth. After that things settled down again in the typing pool, which was probably the best outcome for everyone concerned. John mentioned the Anti-Discrimination Act and suggested the union take things further, but he had already helped me to make a point and I was very grateful to him. I didn't want to make trouble. All I wanted was a fair go.

CHAPTER 18

As a young adult, music continued to be the backbone of my life, as it always has been. Dancing to my favourite songs in a nightclub, I was no different from anyone else - it was the one environment where it didn't matter that I couldn't speak. Work might have defined my days but music defined who I was - with my growing self-assurance and my sassy moves I was everyone's equal on the dance floor.

It would be fair to say that I really 'found my feet' at the Shellharbour Workers Club dances on Friday nights, where The Tornadoes were the resident band. Dancing with Veronica in Sydney's discos had bolstered my confidence and it didn't take me long to make a bunch of new friends at Shelly's. The Tornadoes played top ten hits as well as a few old favourites and there was even a regular barn dance that almost everyone got up for. For me, it was a good way to meet people and to dance with the guys I fancied without being too forward. Every now and then there would be a guy that didn't want to let me go, and we would dance by ourselves in the middle of the circle. During the barn dance the band would pick the best dancers, and they would win a bottle of champagne. The 'champagne' was actually summer wine but it was nice and sweet and by that stage of the evening we were already too happy to care.

After sleeping off any Friday night excess, the Windang Bowling Club became my club of choice on Saturday nights. There were other clubs that had live bands too, but my neighbours Haley, Sharnice and Sheree already went to WBC, so I started going with them. The club was just on the other side of the Lake Illawarra estuary, across the Windang Bridge. There was the same friendly atmosphere as at Shelly's, but it was a different group of friends, and it was busier - we'd often pull two or three tables together, depending on the number of us who were there on the night. A few of the Warilla Gorillas football team players and some of the men from the Warilla Fire Station were also regulars, and my lack of speech didn't seem to bother anyone. Everyone caught on with my slang sign-language and my old notepad. By the time the music started playing you couldn't hear anyone talk anyway, so I was in my element.

Every long weekend WBC would put on a theme night. One time we had a 50s night where we all dressed up in full-skirted dresses and ponytails. Then there was a circus night where we dressed up as animals, and a gender-bender night where the guys dressed as girls, and vice versa. I borrowed a football shirt from Sharnice's brother and drew a moustache on my top lip. I don't think I made much of a fella, but we all had heaps of fun.

On New Year's Eve 1979 my cousin Ian came down from Queensland for a short stay. He got on well with my friends and we all danced the night away. We were totally intoxicated by midnight and us girls went around the club kissing every male in sight. I guess we were young enough to get away with it. I'm not sure that it would work now.

After the last bar call was made we left the club and headed to Pinocchio's for pizza and hot chocolate. Yep, pizza and hot chocolate after drinking copious quantities of summer wine and a large number of colourful cocktails. We were making so much noise, singing and laughing, that the proprietor told us to quieten down or he would call the police. Of course, that's all it took for Sharnice and Sheree to get even louder. They called the poor man a liar. They said they didn't believe he would call the police on New Year's Eve, and Sharnice told him his nose was growing. I felt a bit sorry for him but it was pretty funny at the same time.

When the police duly arrived everyone blamed me. They thought it was hilarious when the constable tried to question me. It was only when he threatened to arrest me that Ian did the right thing and told them why it couldn't have been me. I think the police already knew something was going on because Haley was rolling around the floor, nearly wetting herself.

In the end they let us go with a warning and told us to go straight home. Oh, and they told me not to make so much noise next time, or they would have to do something about it. Haley was still in hysterics as we went our separate ways that night. "It's all your fault," she yelled as she walked away. "You're too noisyyyyyyy!"

A few weeks later I was held back at WBC, helping my friend Mallory pull herself together after she'd had a tiff with her boyfriend. Usually I'd share a taxi home with Haley but on this occasion I missed my ride. Sheree had already left with her boyfriend, and Sharnice was going out with one of the guys in the band, so she was spoken for. When Mallory's brother came to pick her up I didn't think quickly enough to ask for a lift. It was only after their car took off that I realised everyone else had left and I was alone. Luckily the door man at the club was still around to call me a taxi.

When the taxi came it was a new driver that I hadn't seen before. I showed him the note with my address that I always carried, and he looked at me oddly. He was a new Australian and he seemed to think I was deaf. It had been a long night already, and I couldn't be bothered explaining so I just nodded. I was looking out of the window when I heard him call back to base. I thought he said he was clocking off for the night, but I assumed he meant he would clock off *after* he dropped me home.

But instead of turning right towards Warilla, when we come to Shellharbour Road, the taxi driver turned *left*, towards Wollongong. I was frozen for a minute, not sure what to do. Then he reached over and stroked my cheek. "Pretty lady, so pretty, what a pity," he said. I didn't know what was happening but I didn't like it. I gestured for him to stop, but he wouldn't. He turned down a side street that I knew led to the beach. The beach in Windang is surrounded by thick bushland with walkways where the bush has been cut back to access the shore. In the dark you can't see your own hand if you hold it up in front of your face.

The driver pulled up on the sand near one of these walkways and I panicked. I don't think it had ever really hit home before, how helpless I was in a situation like this. I pushed him away and tried to scream but of course no sound came out. I shudder to think what might have happened if it hadn't been for the sheer luck of the headlights that suddenly came up behind us and reflected in the rear vision mirror, shining into the driver's eyes. It's now or never, I thought. I pushed the door open and ran.

My heart felt as if it was going to explode in my chest. The taxi drove past me a few times but he didn't see me as I kept close to the bushes along the side of the beach. I lost my shoes somewhere along the way and when I made it to the highway I hung around in the shadows for a while, waiting to see if he was still around. Then I ran helter-skelter across Windang Bridge. It wasn't until I was over the bridge that I felt a bit safer - I still had a way to walk, but I knew I could make it now.

When I finally got home I realised that my feet were all cut up. I would have to think of some excuse to tell Mum, I thought. I couldn't tell her what really happened. She might not want me to go out again and I couldn't *not* go out dancing - that would be worse than anything. In the end I stayed quiet about the whole thing. After all, I thought, he hadn't really done me any harm, that driver; he had just scared the living daylights out of me and given me another phobia: taxis. I never used taxis after that night. Not unless someone was with me. Buses I would take by myself, but taxis, no way.

***

Throughout this period, my job at the DSS office in Wollongong had settled down and was ticking along. One day I was asked to translate for a deaf client. This wasn't as silly as it might sound - the department knew I sometimes communicated using a kind of sign language; I just didn't do it properly. So when this opportunity came up I decided to learn sign language professionally. My thinking was that I could improve my own communication skills and also interpret for the deaf community at work.

I started to look into learning sign language but in those days there were no courses in Wollongong - I had to teach myself through books, which was hard. But then I heard about a local deaf youth group. I found out that they sometimes gathered at one of the clubs in town, so I decided to learn sign language from them, and that's how I met Gail. Gail's story was similar to mine. She became deaf after complications with Meningitis when she was thirteen years old, but despite her loss of hearing, she was still good at talking. She sometimes stumbled on words and she had that deep-sounding voice that some deaf people have when speaking, but we soon found we made a very good team - she could speak for me, and I could listen for her.

Gail took me along to the deaf youth group in Wollongong, where I made some other deaf friends. Some of them were quite amused that I wasn't joining them because I was deaf, but because I had no voice. When I went out with the group, they would sometimes ask me what other people were saying. It's amazing what you hear when other people think you are deaf, but suffice to say that I only told them the good things.

One evening we all went to see Les Misérables, where I learned that the trick for them was to know the story before going to the show. The deaf still have eyes, of course, and like everyone else in the audience the group loved watching the spectacle of movement and colour. I noticed that they could also feel vibrations from the music, and were aware of the reactions of the people around them. And some of them, depending on the level of their deafness, could pick up snippets of sound. There was a bit of confusion as to the title of the musical because it was French. We ended up calling it 'The Miserable Ones', but even in English I began to appreciate how difficult pronunciation can be. When we visited Circular Quay, for example, I had to teach them to say 'key' and not 'quaaay'.

One of my other friends at this time was Kim Barry. Like me, Kim loved dancing, and she would come out clubbing with us now and then. I'll never know exactly how it happened but Kim was murdered one night in early 1981. It seemed to be a crime of passion but it was a bit hard to tell with Kim, as she liked everybody and everyone liked her.

I will never forget hearing the news when they found Kim's body. I was on holiday in Coolangatta at the time. I was getting ready to go out, and was standing in front of the mirror with my hairdryer when the news came on. I heard her name and thought no, it can't be our Kim Barry, there must be another one. But as I turned off the hairdryer and stopped to watch the TV, I realised it *was* her - she had been chopped up and dumped near the lookout at Jamberoo Mountain. I just stood there in a state of shock. I remember thinking how beautiful Jamberoo was; too beautiful to be the scene of such an atrocious crime.

I didn't know what to do. I couldn't just pick up the phone and call anyone. I had to wait for the newspapers to come out the next day to find out the details. And then I had to wait to get home before I could share my grief with Gail and the others. It wasn't a good holiday that year.

Kim's death was the talk of the town when I got back to Wollongong. It shook us all up. None of us had imagined something like this could happen, but after that we were all careful about who we went home with. Kim's murderer, Graham Potter, had lured her from the nightclub back to his flat where he bludgeoned her before cutting off her fingers and her head.

It was a gruesome story. Kim's parents had been out of town for the night and she'd decided to make the most of her freedom by going out herself, leaving her younger brother at home. Kim's friend Donna met her at the movies and then they shared a bottle of Leibfrau wine at the Crown Gardens, a disco where we all used to go dancing. Donna wasn't feeling great so she went home, having made sure that Kim had enough money for a taxi.

Potter was out on his buck's night when he saw Kim at the Crown Gardens. They already knew each other, but I don't think Kim knew he was engaged to be married. So she went back to his place with him and that's where everything unravelled. During the murder trial Potter said he was innocent and claimed that two unknown men in dark glasses had turned up unannounced and asked to 'speak' with Kim that night. He made out that it was drug related, but we knew Kim as a clean living girl. She liked a glass of wine and a good dance but she wasn't into anything else.

The police couldn't establish a motive for him to kill her, but they didn't buy Potter's story either. There were just too many inconsistencies. For a start, he claimed that the two men in dark glasses had killed Kim in his living room, whereas forensics proved she was murdered in the spare bedroom. And then the hacksaw that was used to dismember her was found along with other evidence at his parents' house. None of it added up. Maybe Potter himself was on drugs? Two years after he was eventually released, he was linked to a massive ecstasy deal with the Calabrian mafia worth hundreds of millions of dollars, so it wouldn't surprise me if he was high on something that night. Maybe he was hoping to get lucky with Kim, to have a fling before he tied the knot with his fiancée. But Kim wasn't like that. She was easy going but she was a good person. I still don't like to think about it too much but I can only guess that she refused his advances and that Potter went crazy.

As time passed by, the sign language that I learned from my friends in the deaf youth group was formalised as 'AusLan'. 1981 was the International Year of Disabled Persons, bringing disability rights into the public eye, and resulting in the publication of the first Auslan dictionary, among other things. Prince Charles visited Australia as a patron of disabilities, and the idea that the deaf of the world could all communicate in one language gained traction. There's still a degree of 'slang' of course, but sign language is much more standardised and easier to learn than it used to be.

In any case, I guess the trauma that we all shared with Kim's murder was too painful, and I lost contact with Gail and the others when I moved to Canberra. Some time later, however, I read in a newspaper that Gail had recovered her hearing. She was one of the first people in Wollongong to have the new cochlear ear implant. We may not have stayed in contact but I'll always feel a sense of connection with Gail. She and I were the same age, more or less, when each of us experienced a loss of communication. Then, eventually, we each regained those faculties. It was almost as if we mirrored each other's stories.

As for Graham Potter, I read recently that now, more than thirty five years after all this happened, he is Australia's most wanted fugitive! After somehow serving a reduced sentence for Kim's murder and then being implicated in the biggest ecstasy seizure in history, he skipped bail on another murder charge and is currently believed to be on the run, possibly somewhere in northern NSW. There is a $100,000 reward on offer for information leading to his capture.

CHAPTER 19

Mum used to get the Illawarra Mercury newspaper every day, so when she saw an ad for the Cliff Richard Fan Club of Australia, she cut it out for me. The Wollongong chapter of the fan club was just a small group but they made up for their numbers with their enthusiasm, and often travelled up to Sydney for meetings, movies and concerts.

I liked Cliff Richard and already had several of his records. I happily went along to the next fan club meeting and had a great night discussing Cliff's upcoming tour with the other club members. I also found out about one of Cliff's charities called Tearfund, or The Evangelical Alliance Relief fund, to use its full name, of which there was an Australian branch called Tear Australia. The fan club had been raising funds for Tear Australia and were going to present Cliff with a cheque during his next tour.

I wasn't too interested in Tear at the beginning of my involvement with the fan club. I was still politically naïve and I believed that the poor people of the world should be looked after by their governments. My thoughts were pretty simple: why should *we* give charity for their upkeep if their own societies didn't? That kind of logic. As I learned more about the way the world really is, however, I began to change my tune.

Tear focuses on underprivileged people in developing countries and in places that are inundated with refugees. As a Christian organisation, Tear asserts that God has particular care for the poor and for those who suffer as victims of injustice. The organisation believes in helping people to help themselves and, as such, Tear workers often volunteer overseas to help with education in health, agriculture and other basic needs. Any wages earned are minimal. For staff, volunteers and partners, working for Tear is a labour of love.

As I became more involved with Tear's activities I began to see that what we were doing, helping the needy to build or rebuild their lives, was a great blessing in itself. For much of my life Christianity had been misrepresented to me in terms of fear and guilt.

Finally I was learning some of the true virtues of my faith. Despite my own trials I began to understand how privileged my life was, compared to so many people in the world. I always had a good bed to sleep in and food on my table, for a start. And the fact that I lived in a prosperous country was largely due to luck and luck alone. Things would be quite different if I had been born in the third world, that's for sure. God only knows what my life would have been like as a mute in those parts.

It took some time, but Tear helped me gain perspective and appreciate all the advantages I had. I began to understand the proverb 'there but for the grace of God go I'.

Several years later, after I eventually recovered my voice, I became the Tear representative for the Cliff Richard Fan Club of Australia. It was a big step for me as it entailed talking in front of large groups of people, as well as putting my beliefs out there.

One of the challenges I encountered was that when I presented videos of Cliff visiting impoverished places, many fan club members would want to fast-forward to the scenes where Cliff was talking. "How do you know what he is talking about if you don't watch the whole thing?" I asked on one occasion. "Oh, it's okay," a young woman replied. "We just like listening to his voice - we'll still donate to Tear."

"You have it the wrong way around," I objected. "Cliff made this video to show us the desperate lives these people are living. It's not *about* him." Donations were important I explained, but an understanding of circumstances can be even more valuable. With that understanding we could pass Cliff's message on and help spread awareness.

I couldn't really blame Cliff's fans. A few years earlier I'd been just the same - naïve and largely uninformed. They meant well and it was my job, after all, to represent Tear. But sometimes it was difficult to remain patient. Poor Cliff. If I got frustrated, he must have got frustrated too, right?

The fan club insisted on giving Cliff their fundraising cheques in person, so that each time he visited our fair shores they would have a good excuse to meet with him and take photos. They would give him cheques in Australian dollars and then I would retrieve these cheques from his manager and send them to the Tear office in Melbourne to bank.

Over the years I organised several Tear projects with the Cliff Richard Fan Club and raised a lot of money with them, but I never asked to meet Cliff myself. Oh, I was tempted, but I just couldn't do it. Anyway, as things unfolded I ended up seeing more of him than most of his fans.

***

I went along to several of Cliff's concerts with Michelle, who was a hobby photographer. Michelle took photos of Cliff to sell and would donate the proceeds to Tear. She also had contacts in the travel industry who made our travel arrangements to coincide with Cliff's tours. Sometimes we'd stay in the same hotel as Cliff and I'd see him in the dining room at breakfast, or in the afternoon, taking refreshments after playing tennis. But I never bothered him. One night I was at the bar when he walked in and took a seat near me. I thought of saying hello but I'd been around long enough to know that it only takes one person to recognise a celebrity and then every Tom, Dick and Harry would come out of the woodwork, and there would go that relaxing drink he was having.

The last time I saw Cliff was in a hotel in Perth. It was late in the evening and I'd just been talking with Roger, his manager. "Cliff will be down in a minute," Roger said. "We're going to the airport to pick up a friend." I was too tired to really take in what he was saying. Roger had never told me anything about Cliff's itinerary before, so I just thought it was nice of him to be going out so late to pick someone up.

When I walked to the lifts to go back to my room Roger was at the door of the hotel, waiting with Cliff's car. I waved to him and turned to get into the lift which had just 'pinged'. When the doors opened, there was Cliff, right in front of me! He raised his hand as though he recognised me and was going to say something, but then out of the corner of my eye I saw a flash - a camera lens was poking through the shrubbery of the indoor garden.

I looked Cliff right in the eyes and said "Run!" What surprised me is that he actually did. Like a bolt of lightning he was across the lobby and out to the car, where Roger had the door open and ready. Damn it, damn it, damn it, I thought. Cliff had been going to say hello to me! All these years I had secretly wanted to meet him and then, when I finally had the chance, I told him to run away. Good one, Marie.

I sometimes wonder if Cliff remembers that night in Perth. Or the night he was at the bar and I let him be, or the day at the swimming pool when he was sunbathing and I moved the sun brolly over so the paparazzi wouldn't be able to get a clear view of him. In any case, I never got another chance to meet him after that. And he changed his management team soon afterwards, so I didn't see Roger again either.

Years later, after multiple illnesses and surgery, I had to give up my work with Tear. But I still listen to Cliff's records, and I still hold him partly responsible for my parents bringing me to Australia in the first place. 'Summer Holiday' - I'm sure that song must have influenced their decision to migrate!

Back in 1981 this was all in the future, of course, and I had no idea that my involvement with Tear would eventually lead me to Cliff Richard himself. I was still completely mute, and the thought that I might one day recover my voice seemed more remote than ever.

But I didn't dwell on it anymore. For better or worse I didn't think about the future that much at all. I was twenty one years old. I lived for the weekend, for music and for dancing.

At that time my first husband, Ed, worked in Parliament House as a speechwriter for the incumbent prime minister, Malcolm Fraser. Ed visited his family in Nowra every long weekend, and that's how I met him at the Windang Bowling Club, where his brother Doug played in Deja Vu. My friend Sharnice was going out with the guitar player in the band, so we got to know all of them pretty well.

I knew Doug for quite a while before I met Ed, and Doug made it clear that he didn't think it was a good idea for me to go out with his brother. I remember him saying that Ed didn't 'treat his women right', so I'm not sure how me and him became an item, but I do remember him being a good dancer, so maybe I was blinded by his moves or something. At some point he invited me to visit him in Canberra. I stayed in a hotel as he rented a room in a boarding house and couldn't have people staying over, or so he said.

After a while Ed came to stay the weekend with me in Warilla. We slept in separate rooms, of course; Mum wouldn't have it any other way. Then I met Ed's parents too. His mother, Heloise, was what I would term a 'real lady'. She made scones every afternoon, with homemade jam and cream. She was a very giving person, and thought of everyone else before herself.

Ed and I were married in February 1982, but to this day I'm not really sure why. I guess I did love him in a way, but it definitely wasn't the *right* way. I don't remember him ever really kissing me or holding me the way a lover's supposed to. At first I thought he was just being a gentleman but once we were married I learned otherwise. On our wedding night we tried to have sex but he hurt me too much and we had to stop. He wasn't very nice about it. He told me that none of his other girlfriends had found it difficult so it had to be my 'problem'.

After that we didn't try again. On our honeymoon in Surfers Paradise, Ed slept in until after lunch every day, so we never even got the chance to go sightseeing. I should have got the marriage annulled then and there, but of course I didn't. Looking back on it, the reality was that we were a terrible match, but I guess we looked good on paper. Ed had a great job and he could make a good impression when he wanted to. Mum was besotted with him because he brought her flowers when we visited, and he would also bring Dad a bottle of Drambuie or something. My parents thought they had the perfect gentleman as a son-in-law, but they didn't know what things were really like. Ed just couldn't relax, for a start. As soon as he got up he would shower and get fully dressed - shoes, socks, everything. I never saw him wear shorts or even thongs in summer. Maybe it was the boarding school upbringing he'd had, or maybe the pressure of his job? I don't know.

After the honeymoon we moved in together in a small apartment. Ed went back to work at Parliament House and I transferred to the Department of Social Security in the Silverton Building in Civic - the heart of Canberra, if Canberra can be said to have a heart. It wasn't what I would call an exciting life. We went out to a few dinners with Ed's friends but I didn't really fit in with them. They were all older than me and I always got that condescending smile and a nod of the head that people in politics are so good at. They weren't much interested in me as a person.

Around that time I started getting a lift to work with our next door neighbour, Jenny. Jenny worked in Civic too, so it became routine that we travelled to work together, and we soon became close friends. With such a dull life at home, I was all the happier to spend time with her. Among her many talents, Jenny was a marvel in the kitchen, and she taught me how to make a delicious spaghetti. Mum had always been a meat and potatoes kind of cook, but Jenny turned mealtimes into an adventure.

The apartment we shared began to feel claustrophobic, but Ed worked late hours and often wouldn't get home until I was heading out to work in the mornings, so we ended up avoiding each other most of the time. On the weekends he slept late and then he would go to the club and play the pokies and eat there at the bistro. I'd been learning a few tricks from Jenny but when I tried making dinner for Ed he got angry and said he didn't need anyone to cook for him. I was upset; I think I felt even more rejected by this then by our lack of intimacy. All in all, I really wasn't sure what my role in his life was supposed to be.

Just to be sure, I went to see my GP to learn about my sexual 'problem'. When I explained things the doctor asked me exactly what my husband did before we got to the intercourse on our wedding night. I was embarrassed and didn't know what he meant. He was talking to a girl who had been educated in a Catholic school, after all. I had no real understanding of these things and hadn't even seen a man fully naked before. I had read books like 'Every Woman' and 'The Joy of Sex' but they hadn't made much sense to me. I thought that with the right guy things would just 'happen'. I didn't realise that one has to *make* things happen. Apparently Ed hadn't realised that either, because in all truth he didn't try very hard at all.

As the months went by Ed started drinking more and I saw him less. Then, after eight years of being Australia's prime minister, Malcolm Fraser was succeeded by Bob Hawke, who swept to power in the general election in March 1983. Ed's career prospects took a tumble and his lifestyle reflected his misfortunes. On several mornings I found him passed out in the hallway, so out of it that he hadn't even made it from the front door to the lounge before collapsing.

Ed didn't seem too concerned when I finally told him I wanted to leave, but he asked me to wait a while before we told our families, as he didn't want to upset his parents. So for a few more months we were still living together and visiting our parents on public holidays as if nothing was wrong. On one of these visits his mum told me she was praying for me to get pregnant.

One night shortly afterwards, Ed came into the bedroom, which he usually didn't do. He tried to force himself on me but he couldn't do it. He was too drunk and he fell asleep on top of me. I pushed him off and I went to sleep on the lounge. I decided I'd had enough.

The next day I packed my things and moved into Jenny's place.

As soon as I moved out, Ed said he wanted to go to counselling. It was funny, because I had asked him to go to counselling with me months earlier and he had outright refused. But anyway, since he now seemed to be making an effort, I relented and I went to see a marriage guidance counsellor with him. I kept an open mind during the session, but after listening to us for an hour the counsellor said there was no use staying together, we just weren't compatible.

Ed wasn't happy. He visited my GP and tried to convince him to have me incarcerated, back in a psychiatric hospital. Ed told the doctor that I wasn't in my right mind. He said that I might do harm to myself or others. Luckily for me the GP saw through his lies and that was the end of that.

All in all the marriage lasted three years. During that time Ed drained our joint account to cover his heavy drinking lifestyle and his gambling habit, and in the end I left with only my clothes and personal effects. Ed tried to stop the divorce proceedings from going through by claiming that we were still living together, but I had the proof of my rental receipts at Jenny's place, and the loan I had taken out to buy furniture.

Some years later I met Ed's sister in a shopping centre in Sydney. She told me he had remarried and was living interstate. I was just glad to move on after the divorce and everything else, so I was happy to hear that he was doing well. There's no point holding grudges. However bad our relationship might have been, and despite what was yet to come, I'm glad that things eventually got better for both of us.

Chapter 20

Within three months of moving to Canberra I had been promoted to the position of Typist Supervisor with the Department of Social Security. I knew I had been well trained, but I was still surprised - after some of my previous experiences I hadn't thought my career prospects were much to write home about. With the way things were going in my marriage it was a consolation to be appreciated at work, but I soon realised that being promoted came with a new set of challenges that I hadn't anticipated. And not everyone in the typing pool was happy about it either.

At the time of my promotion the DSS was being modernised. The various sections of the department were merging together and our duty statements were changing accordingly. 'Multiskilling' was the new buzzword. The clerical staff were going to type up their own work, moving forward, and the typists would eventually be integrated into the clerical division. Typewriters, telex machines and data entry processors were all being replaced by computers.

It would happen slowly, over a five year period, but eventually the old typing pool would be no more. The union assured us that no one would lose their jobs as a result of the changes, but in the end the government just waited until people retired and then didn't replace them. It was the start of the union's downfall; they sold us out for technology.

Meanwhile, every staff member had to go to Sydney for instruction courses on how to operate the new computers and how to manage the massive hard drives, that looked a bit like space-age washing machines. We were split up into two groups so that the Canberra office would still be able to operate on a skeleton staff while each group was trained in turn. There were four of us in my team: myself, Kameron, Eva and Larissa. During our six weeks of intensive training I was put up in a serviced apartment on York St, near Sydney HQ and the training centre. It was a secure building with a doorman, and my apartment had a bedroom, an open plan living area and a very big bathroom. I felt like a VIP, staying there.

As a supervisor I was assigned extra training and a higher security clearance than the other girls. It was up to me to monitor and fix any anomalies before they were printed or sent on to HQ, but the training wasn't as difficult as I expected. The things that the new computers could do were incredible. There would be no more re-typing of letters or reports if mistakes were made. Typing was made easy, with a simple backspace button to edit material. We just had to remember to save our files and to back all our work up at the end of the day.

During those six weeks I often thought about the twists and turns of life that had brought me back to Sydney. It had only been a couple of years since I had been living in the RSL house in Kings Cross but I'd been through a lot in that time, including marriage and separation. It felt to me as though everything was different now - I had grown up.

One weekend we decided to have a girls' night out. We thought we'd have a nice dinner somewhere and then go to a nightclub or the theatre. There was only one problem - we didn't have a clue where to go. When we were all ready Eva waved down a taxi and asked the driver to take us somewhere nice. I was still wary of taxi drivers, but there were the four of us, so I told myself there was nothing to worry about. Well, this particular taxi driver must have been laughing all night after he dropped us off at the Jamison Street disco. He said it was very popular and that a buffet dinner was included in the door price. We thought that sounded good, so in we went. At the door there was a $30 entrance fee, which was a bit expensive, but it was Sydney after all - going out in the city is always more expensive than at home.

There was something odd about the Jamison Street nightclub that I couldn't put my finger on at first, but when we were shown to a table I realised what it was - there were no men in the place. Well, maybe that's not too unusual, I thought. The women had probably just come from work like we had. Maybe their husbands or male friends would be joining them later. But then, as one of the waiters came towards us, I noticed something else. He was practically naked! He wore a bow tie around his neck, a G-string, and a little apron tied around his middle. Nothing else.

"Jesus," Eva said, "We're in a strip club!" Larissa's eyes were particularly wide. "I can't stay here," she trilled. "What will my husband say?" I had to silently laugh; what else could I do? 'We can't leave,' I scrawled on my notepad. 'It would be too embarrassing to leave and have them know that we didn't know what we were walking into… Let's stay and see what happens?' It took me a while to get my point across but Kameron came to my aid. "Marie's right," she grinned. "And besides, whatever happens it will be an experience, right?"

It sure was an experience. After we'd eaten and the waiters had plied us with a few drinks everyone was feeling a lot more r..e..l..a..x..e..d. Then the staff moved the buffet away and the lights were dimmed. The women on the other tables started screaming and carrying on as soon as the raunchy music started. The strip show really was entertaining, and much more athletic than I might have imagined. One of the strippers came to our table and gyrated in front of me, but it wasn't really my cup of tea. "Don't you like me?" he asked. "Would you like one of the other guys?" Being me I had to reply in my little notepad while he patiently gyrated. "It's not that I don't like you," I wrote. "But I'd rather be *alone* with a naked man than in the middle of a club!" The girls all burst out laughing when they read that. Later on the stripper came back with a few more clothes on. He gave me a card with his phone number on it. "Get one of your friends here to make the call for you," he suggested.

After an hour or two the strippers packed up and the doors were opened to let guys in. I've often wondered who thought that one up: have a male strip show, get the ladies hot and bothered, and then start the disco and let the men in. Well, it didn't work with us. We just listened to the music and had fun trying to concoct a viable story in case anyone at work found out where we'd been. In the end we decided to stick to the truth, in the unlikely event that we were questioned: we didn't know where to go for a night out so we asked the taxi driver. It doesn't sound too convincing, does it? But that's exactly what happened.

Back at training the following Monday, our instructors kept smirking and giving us strange looks. By lunchtime I'd had enough. 'Okay, out with it,' I wrote. 'What's so funny?' Then I caught Eva's eye and she blushed. Damn, I thought. Not lying about something doesn't mean you have to voluntarily go and *tell* everyone about it. And sure enough, *everyone* at the training centre knew we'd been to a strip show. To top it all off, our colleagues in Canberra seemed to know too. This was the days before the internet and mobile phones, remember. The pigeons must have been busy that weekend!

After six weeks in Sydney we returned to work, expecting to just hop on the computers and take off. But as I soon found, it wasn't that easy. There were still 'teething' issues, and there were several outages and losses of documents as everyone adjusted to the new systems. A lot of time was taken looking up manuals and fixing mistakes. Work had piled up and we were short-staffed and working overtime while the other group was away training. And then I had Beatrice Knowles to worry about.

Beatrice Knowles was a senior member of the typing pool in Canberra at this time. At first I was worried that she might be offended that I got the job of supervisor ahead of her, but Daniel, our regional manager, said that she wasn't qualified as she didn't have my level of experience. On top of that she had told him that she wanted to stay a typist and had refused to be trained in word processing. So I had no idea that anything was amiss.

I only found out that Beatrice was unhappy when Daniel called me into his office and told me that she had lodged a complaint with the Public Service Board and the union. According to Beatrice's statement, I shouldn't have been given the supervisor's position. She argued that by seniority the position should have been hers. Okay, I thought, maybe she's changed her mind about things? But then she went even further, accusing me of having an affair with Daniel to get the job!

My friend Rosie saw what Beatrice was doing, and she stuck up for me. Rosie was a tall stocky woman with long red hair and a lovely laugh. She was always supportive and sympathetic. Without her around I might not even have stayed at work, to be honest, as the investigation of Beatrice's slander was pretty humiliating. Both Daniel and I were interviewed and had to answer the allegations in writing. We were not allowed to communicate with each other, which was difficult as he was my boss. Beatrice had insisted on staying in the typing pool too, so I still had to face her every day. Needless to say, there was a lot of tension in the office during this time. With all the stress I decided to look for a transfer, and I applied for a position with ASIO, the Australian Security Intelligence Organisation. The job was on the Cocos Islands and was for six month stints. Everything would be provided, so all my wages would be saved, and I wouldn't have to pay tax, because the Cocos Islands are 'outside' Australia, and well, ASIO is ASIO - I guess a different set of rules apply to them.

Anyway, just as I was considering the move, the union asked me to file counter-charges against Beatrice. It didn't make everything okay, but it did become clear that *she* was the one discriminating against me, and not the other way around. I didn't want to press any charges, but I asked the union rep to explain to Beatrice that what she was doing was wrong. I forgot about my ASIO application and things at the DSS returned to a kind of normality.

Then one day I got a new project out of the blue. I was used to working late with the backlog of work that we'd had, so I wasn't fazed when I was told that a high security figure called 'the Prof' needed someone to stay back to help him once or twice a month. I had been asked for because of the application I had made for the ASIO job on the Cocos Islands, which I had since forgotten about. Looking back on it, it's obvious they wanted someone who couldn't talk, but at the time it just seemed mysterious and exciting to me. The reports for the Prof had to be typed on telex tape, so the information came out looking like little dots, a bit like Morse code on paper. I was told not to read back or edit any of the documents, and I was advised to only do the work when the other typists had gone home. I usually packaged the completed tape into an envelope and placed it in the bottom drawer of the filing cabinet in the main office, to which I was given a key.

So began my short lived career with ASIO: every few weeks I received a package of documents from a courier and when the other girls had gone home I would type them up. I guess it sounds clandestine and exciting, but I didn't really know what I was transcribing as the information didn't make much sense to me anyway. It was all a bit surreal at the best of times, so when the Prof himself walked in one evening, I didn't initially think much of it.

I don't know what I expected but the Prof was actually a pretty normal looking guy. He looked like he didn't see enough sunlight, but apart from that and the greying sideburns there was nothing unusual about him. He just seemed a bit nervous when I took the envelope from him and he asked if he could pick it up early the next morning.

At that moment I realised that I couldn't even be sure if this actually *was* the Prof, and I began to feel a bit uncomfortable with the break in protocol, especially when he told me not to put the package in the usual place, but rather to leave it on my desk when I was done. "Be sure to telex it right away after you've typed it," he said as he left. Something in his manner struck me as strange, but I just shrugged my shoulders and carried on. Who was I to scrutinise these academics anyway - they're all a bit strange, aren't they?

I opened the envelope and set myself up, and as I typed the characters my first thought was to just to hurry up so I could go home. But something bothered me - something just wasn't right about this assignment. So instead of sending it over the telex machine, like the Prof had asked, I tested the number first: I punched in the number and a few seconds later a response came back with a receiving number and an identification name.

The number and name that came back weren't familiar to me, and the identification tag wasn't even from a government department. Nothing added up. The irregularity of 'the Prof' himself turning up to give me the documentation, instead of sending it via courier. The nervousness of the guy. The fact that he asked me to leave it on my desk for him to pick up. None of it made any sense.

So I didn't leave the package on my desk as he asked; I locked it in the filing cabinet as usual. And I didn't send the telex because I didn't trust the unknown number and identification. I wrote all this down in a statement and left it in the envelope with the written copy and the tape I had made. I thought I would get in early the next day so I could be there when Daniel arrived. Then I could tell him what had happened and we could sort it out.

But the next morning when I arrived at work, Daniel was already in his office with two men in suits. My heart rate doubled. Suits. It never bodes well for me when there are suits involved.

Daniel called me in and before I'd even sat down the two men started questioning me about the Prof. They asked what he had said and what he looked like. They wanted as much detail as possible. Then, as they were leaving, one of them turned to me. He had a deep voice. "Did you read any of the text?" he asked. I shook my head. "Hmmmm," he said. Then he nodded at me and Daniel and he and his partner left. Just like that.

After they had entered the lift and I was sure they weren't coming back, my heart finally stopped racing. 'What was all that about?' I asked Daniel in my quickest scribble. 'Did they take the envelope? Did I do the right thing, not sending it?'

"What envelope?" Daniel replied. "Nothing happened, Marie," he said. "You went home at five o'clock last night like you usually do. You didn't see anyone or communicate with anyone at all. And if you did by chance read any of the contents of the envelope that didn't exist, then you certainly don't remember any of it. Do you understand?" I breathed out slowly and nodded.

I never heard anything more about it, but I suppose I must have done the right thing or else I would have been in trouble for not obeying orders. Maybe the Prof, or whoever he was, was acting out of place? Maybe he was sending the information to another source, to the media or to some other third party? It's frustrating being left in the dark, but no matter how much I speculate I guess I'll never know what was really going on. Don't you just hate those mysteries that can't be solved?

CHAPTER 21

I might have had more than my fair share of experiences in general, but as an independent woman in her early twenties I still hadn't enjoyed a good relationship with a man. My marriage with Ed had been a farce, and I felt like I was missing out. So when I met Neil I thought he was my ticket to the fun and romance that all those Hollywood movies had taught me to expect. I had no idea that the darkest chapter of my life was about to begin.

My Canberran friend Kameron and her boyfriend Dominic set me up with Neil. It was Dominic's birthday, and we all went out on a double date to the local Chinese restaurant in Civic. I eyed Neil up between courses. He didn't look bad but I was just going through my divorce with Ed at the time, and I really didn't want any more complications.

Over the duration of the meal I found out that Neil was in the same situation as me - he was also going through a divorce and wasn't looking for commitment. Neil was a soldier, like Dominic, and he only had a few weeks in Canberra before being posted to Sydney. After the double date we decided that we liked each other's company enough to have a casual 'fling' while his time in Canberra lasted. Then we would part ways. Such are the best laid plans of mice and men.

At this time I was living in a small villa in Queanbeyan, having moved on from Jenny's place. Neil would come over and we would spend the weekends dining out at local restaurants and going to see drive-in movies. I fell eagerly into the 'fling' and had a good time with Neil in those few weeks.

After my failure of a marriage with Ed I think I was proving to myself that I could have a normal relationship with a man.

Shortly after Neil left, however, I felt something wasn't right. I kept feeling nauseous and weak. It might seem obvious, reading this now, but at the time I couldn't make sense of it, especially as I was on 'the pill'. So I went to see my GP again and lo and behold, I found out I was pregnant. This revelation was all the more unsettling as I'd still been having my periods, albeit not as heavily as usual. I'd naturally assumed this was because of the 'placebo week' pills - the break in the contraceptive hormone program that results in withdrawal bleeding.

Neil was the only man besides Ed that I had been with, so it was obvious that he was the father. But what should I do? On the one hand it had been a 'no strings' relationship, and on the other hand I didn't want to be a single mother or one of those women who married 'shotgun' because they were pregnant. I wasn't sure how to handle my new situation and I needed time to sort myself out, but all the while the 'morning sickness' got worse. I vomited every day, at all hours. I even had to stop the bus a few times so I could get off to throw up. I should've stopped drinking those lime milkshakes - they didn't look too good the second time around. On top of everything else it didn't take the girls at the office long to realise I was pregnant, and of course Beatrice Knowles seized the opportunity to spread the rumour that our manager Daniel was the father!

At this time I was still casually involved with what might be called the 'dark side' of Christianity. I had stayed in touch with my friend Chris and would occasionally accompany him to coven meetings. I was never comfortable with the more ritualistic aspects of the coven, but I enjoyed the social functions and I became friends with some of the more easy-going members, including a charismatic young man who called himself Luc.

Luc was very charming and had a knack for making everyone feel welcome. He was tall, muscular and dark haired, and nothing at all like you'd expect a Satanist to be. I think he was born Luke, but changed the spelling of his name to make an impression. In any case, he was actually a really nice guy. Even when he talked about Satan, it wasn't threatening in any way. It was more like he thought it was funny that Christians were so uptight.

According to Luc, Lucifer was once the brother of Jesus and used to sit together with God in heaven. Luc argued that it wasn't a stretch of the imagination, if you accept that Jesus is the son of God, to accept that Lucifer was also His son. They just had different personalities, as is the case with most siblings. Lucifer wanted more of a life and wished for greater involvement in the human world. God disapproved, and, long story short, Lucifer was cast out of heaven with some of his groupies.

Morgan was an acquaintance of Luc's that I met in Canberra. She worked for a women's health organisation and when she learned I was pregnant she wanted to talk to me about my 'options'. She said I didn't need to go through with having the baby if I wasn't happy with my situation, and that I should consider the alternatives. She made sense, what with the sickness I had and the absence of the father of my child - how did I think things were going to pan out?

To say I was conflicted by all this would be a huge understatement. Morgan's arguments were persuasive but I knew in my heart that I wanted the baby. It's unnerving how life can change course so quickly. Just a few months earlier I had been slamming God, saying He didn't exist, but now I was thinking of Him more and more. Once there is someone else to look after, my body was telling me, one's outlook can shift dramatically. A baby was God's gift - everyone knew that. So maybe, just maybe, He didn't despise me after all?

Morgan called me one evening when I was wrestling with my conscience. She told me that there was a coven 'get together' in Sydney that weekend, and she asked me to come along. She said it would do me good to be around friends and people who understood me. It didn't sound ominous at the time but I think she used that exact phrase: "people who understand you".

I didn't really feel up to it, but in the end I decided to go along, thinking the distraction might be a relief. I can't begin to count the number of times I've re-lived the 'if onlys' of that decision. If only I could have seen what was coming. If only I hadn't been so naïve. If only I had just stayed home...

Morgan picked me up from my place that Saturday afternoon. I'd had a few days off work that week, during which the vomiting had eased a little, but I still felt exhausted and I had to ask her to stop a couple of times on the drive up to Sydney, so that I could get some fresh air. Somewhere near Mittagong I fell asleep.

I only woke up when we arrived at a large house, somewhere in the city suburbs. I don't know exactly where it was , but it was a very grand place with a nice water fountain and a spacious garden. I didn't recognise anyone when we went inside. I was a little disappointed that Luc didn't seem to be around but someone gave me a glass of punch and I did my best to be sociable.

Evening was only just falling but I began to feel more exhausted than ever. At first I thought it was still just the sickness but I felt stranger and stranger, and I had to keep shaking myself to stay awake. When Morgan noticed the state I was in she settled me in an armchair and put a blanket over my knees. "Don't worry about it," she said. "You just have a snooze and I'll wake you when we're going home." Her voice seemed distant as I struggled with my notebook. 'Morgan, I really don't feel right,' I wrote in slow, difficult words. 'Something's wrong - it's not just the morning sickness, it's something else...' Everything seemed to stretch away from me as I wrote. It was like I was heading into a tunnel and hearing the echoes of people speaking, rather than their actual voices. I could see shapes and hear sounds but nothing made any sense. I felt as if I was floating.

Suddenly I needed to vomit again. I dragged myself up on my feet and stumbled to the toilets. I knew that they weren't too far away; just through the archway, into the hallway, and through the door... But it seemed to be an endless journey, every step seemed to take an eternity. The house was half empty. What a strange party, I thought, as I waded through the thickening air. Where is everybody? I just made it to the toilet in time to throw up. Then I slumped to the floor and passed out.

After a while I became dimly aware of movement. I was being carried upstairs. I thought I could hear Morgan's voice somewhere in the distance. "She's awake," I heard her say. "No she isn't," another voice contested. "Lady K will have seen to that." Was I dreaming? I'd never heard of this Lady K. The voices seemed to be remote but very loud. And I couldn't move a muscle. I felt a surge of anxiety but there was nothing I could do. My body was already too far away. "Are you sure?" That was Morgan again. "Don't worry. She might stir but she won't remember anything," the other voice boomed.

My vision blurred and darkened as I tried to make out where I was and what was going on. I told myself to wake up, I must be in one of my nightmares. But I couldn't wake up. The nightmare went on and on. I felt pain inside and an intense cramp. Then everything closed in on me and I slipped under the surface of consciousness again.

When I came to, all signs of the party had been cleared up. The room that I found myself in looked just like any other suburban lounge room. A severe looking lady that I didn't recognise came over to me, her heels clicking in her wake. "You've had a bad turn, dear," she said. "Just lie still and I'll get you a glass of water." I felt confused. I looked down. My thighs were streaked with blood and I had a large pad wadded between my legs. I started hyperventilating in panic but the woman just shook her head, ever so slowly. "Don't cause a fuss, dear," she said. "You didn't want the baby anyway. Now he has fulfilled his destiny."

When the woman returned with a tray of sandwiches and a glass of water I just stared at her. I wasn't hungry at all. I was still computing what she had said; I was too stunned to think about anything else. The party, the darkness, the pain - none of it made any sense. What destiny was she talking about? Why was I bleeding?

The stress and confusion weren't helping with the disorientation I felt. I wanted to make sense of what had happened, but before I could order my thoughts the woman said I had to get my things together because I was being picked up. When I found my notebook I asked where Morgan was, but she didn't answer. Then, when I asked for Luc, she looked oddly at me. "He doesn't know you're here," she said.

Just then a familiar voice came from the doorway. It was Ed, my ex-husband. He'd grown a moustache and my first thought was that it didn't suit him, but what on earth was he doing here? "Hurry up and get your bag," he said, as he glanced me over. "I'm taking you to your mother's so you can recuperate."

I wanted to scream the questions that were in my mind. *What are you doing here, Ed? Where are we? What the hell is going on?* But Ed was on his own trip, oblivious to the state I was in. "I haven't told her that you've had a miscarriage, so you won't need to explain anything," he said. *What? Miscarried?* I might have been confused but I knew that whatever just happened wasn't a miscarriage. And hang on - Mum didn't even know I was pregnant in any case. I had been too tied up in my own emotional turmoil to tell her. I got into the car with Ed but I was too confused to understand any of it.

Ed drove me to Warilla, as he said he would, but he didn't speak at all on the journey. When I tried to find out how he knew where I was, or how he knew the people at the house, or where Morgan had gone, he had no answers for me. He just dropped me off at Mum's place and told her that I needed to rest. Mum looked at me hopefully. "So, are you two thinking of getting back together?" she asked. It was too weird. I couldn't process any more. I pushed past her into the house. I went straight to my old room with the familiar paisley curtains and I crawled into bed. It was only then that the full force of what had happened came home to me. I pulled the blankets over my head and wept an ocean of silent tears for the loss of my child.

I never saw Ed again after that night. I still don't know how he was involved in the whole thing. As far as I knew he didn't know anything about the coven. But then I remembered how cunning he was. I remembered how he would drive us to Sunday Mass when we visited his parents: Ed would stay in the car and get me to look inside the church to see which priest was officiating so we could tell his parents it was Father such and such or so and so. With this information he would dupe his parents into thinking we had attended Mass. Maybe his duplicity didn't stop there.

My thoughts revisited the fact that Ed had tried to have me committed. Was it possible for a man to be so hell bent on revenge? I couldn't answer that question then and I still don't know, but it could be that sometimes it's better not to have all the answers.

Soon after this ordeal I was seconded to the Bondi Junction office of the DSS. After my adventure with the suits and the Prof, the department was only too happy to transfer me. I had been thinking of asking for a job in Nowra when I found out I was pregnant, but now, after everything that had happened, I didn't mind being further from home.

It was in Bondi Junction that I started feeling sick and tired again. At first I put it down to the stress and the heartache, but then the GP I went to found a growth in my uterus. She was quite excited when she told me I was pregnant. 'No,' I wrote, 'I can't be!' I explained that I had lost a baby just weeks ago and hadn't had any sexual contact since then. But we went ahead with an ultrasound and there indeed was a foetus. When I saw the little angel on the screen I was ecstatic. I thought it was a reprieve. I've been given a second chance, I thought. I'm going to have a baby after all!

The next day I had an appointment with a gynaecologist who said it was rare, but it can happen. When twins aren't identical and have their own sacs, you can lose one and not the other. I was over the moon about it - I felt as if all my sins had been forgiven.

But it wasn't to be. I lost that baby too. A few weeks later I went for a check up and there was no heartbeat. I was admitted to hospital straight away, but it was too late; I had to say goodbye to my second unborn child. I didn't know if it was God or the Devil or just life in general that was punishing me, but I was distraught. A glimpse of redemption had been lost. I was beyond broken hearted.

CHAPTER 22

After losing my unborn babies I was sure I was done with God, once and for all. I had already denounced Him at coven meetings, as I had been asked to, but now I felt further away from Him than ever. I began to see the bible as nothing but a tool of manipulation; a means by which the Church could remain all powerful. The bible quote 'Slaves, obey your earthly masters with respect and fear and sincerity of heart, just as you would obey Christ' took on a new and cynical meaning in my heart.

I suppose I floated aimlessly for a while. I went through the motions at work, first in Bondi Junction and then back in Canberra. I moved into a new apartment near my friend Jenny and I lived day to day, but I was far from happy. The truth was that I didn't know which way to turn. I was mourning the loss of my children. All I saw were dead ends in every direction.

The last time I saw Luc was at an Equinox celebration. I hadn't had anything to do with the coven since that night at the house in Sydney, but I was feeling lost and I didn't have anywhere else to be. I thought he might be able to help. As soon as he saw me, however, Luc drew me away from the others. We walked outside under the gunmetal moon and I thought he might be going to answer all my unanswerable questions. I wanted to ask him where he'd been that terrible night, and why he didn't warn me. Didn't he know about it? Didn't anyone tell him?

Luc's eyes seemed to shine with a light of their own as I waited for him to speak, but he was quiet for some time - it was as though he was struggling with a crisis of conscience. Maybe there were some things he was just not allowed to talk about. We stood together in a heavy silence and eventually he sighed as he seemed to make some kind of decision. He brushed my hair back and placed his palm on my forehead. "You need to go, Marie," he said slowly, looking deep into my eyes. "You're not one of us." It felt like a rejection but in my heart I knew his words were true. Luc walked me back to my car, avoiding the other coven members on the way. "Go now, before it's too late," he whispered as I got in to leave.

He had beautiful eyes, Luc did. I think I would have done anything for those eyes, but I honestly believe that he only ever wanted the best for me, even if others might have meant me harm. So I took his advice and left the coven for good that night, afraid of what I might see if I stayed. I was in a bit of a state when I reached home but I realised I needed to start pulling myself together. I had followed my curiosity too far and I had ended up forsaken. It was time to look after myself. It was time to find my proper place in the world.

It was Mum's birthday in October, so that year I decided to go down to Warilla for the weekend. I thought I could take Mum and Dad out to the club for dinner, as we hadn't done that for a while. As long as I didn't have to play darts, anything was fine with me, and I thought the trip might do me good. I made some mixtape compilations and I remember playing all my favourite songs on the three hour drive - I guess some habits just don't go away, even when the whole world changes around you.

While I was in Warilla I developed a sore throat, which was unusual because I hadn't had any cold or flu symptoms since becoming mute, more than a decade earlier. I thought I must be coming down with something, but I didn't know the half of it. After celebrating Mum's birthday I drove back to Canberra and Jenny dropped me off at work on Monday morning, as usual.

"Morning 'Rie, how is ya today?" Alan asked as I passed the switchboard. Alan had been in a car accident and was wheelchair-bound. He was a bit of a larrikin, and since he'd found out that I wasn't a fan of Country and Western music he would always sing 'Home on the Range', just to rile me. Oh no, I thought, as I walked on, please don't start singing that dreadful song again,

I can't face it today. Too late: "Home, home on the range, where the deer and the antelope plaaayyyyyy," Alan sang, with a mischievous grin. "Where seldom is heard a discouraging word…" I turned and walked backwards, signing to him as I went. 'One day, Alan… just you wait…'

I picked up the messages that had been left in my in-tray and headed over to my desk in the word processing area. I waved to the other girls and, having received the usual hateful glare from Beatrice, went about my day as normal. But later that morning I was interrupted in the middle of typing a report - the persistent tickle in my throat had worsened. I stood up to get a drink of water but suddenly felt I was going to be sick, so I ran to the ladies toilets. As soon as I reached the basins I started retching. Blood gushed out of my mouth and the floor started heaving like a swarm of maggots in a dog's dinner bowl. I hung onto the sink in case I passed out.

My breath came in gasps and my head was pounding. My legs turned to jelly. I could feel something at the back of my mouth, but it seemed to be stuck. My first thought was that I'd coughed up something from my innards, and I wasn't game enough to try to spit it out. As soon as the mirrors stopped swimming in front of me, I grabbed some paper towels to cover my mouth and ran back out to the foyer, almost crashing into Alan's desk in the process. I scribbled on a piece of paper for him to call an ambulance.

The doctors at the hospital were perplexed. They didn't seem to know what was going on. The bleeding had stopped but I was terrified, and I wasn't great with doctors even at the best of times, remember. When they finally talked me into opening my mouth they found a hard lump at the back of my throat, but they didn't know what it was and they were reluctant to treat me until a specialist had been called. I must have been the topic of the day, as doctor after doctor came in to examine me.

Eventually I was given something to numb my nerves and one of the surgeons removed the object. It turned out to be a 1959 Australian threepence coin. Yes, a coin! It was as much of a surprise to me as anyone else. No one could have guessed it. I had no idea how I could have swallowed a coin without knowing about it in the first place, and besides, threepenny coins had been out of circulation since decimalisation in 1966, long before I arrived in Australia.

It didn't make any sense, but that's what it was. I suppose the surgeon was as gentle as possible, but after twelve years of being lodged against my vocal chords the coin had been partially enveloped by mucosa or some other connective tissue. It felt like the inside of my larynx was being ripped out of my throat, even with the anaesthetic.

After the coin was removed I was shaking all over and felt very cold. The nurses gave me something to calm me down, but I was freaked out. There were strange noises coming from my mouth. I hadn't talked since I was thirteen years old, so I couldn't understand how the sounds were being made. I didn't believe it was me. I thought someone was mimicking me, making fun of me.

The specialist that eventually came to see me was dumbfounded. "What? She hasn't talked for *how many* years?" he asked. He had to double check several times. "Are you sure?" he asked. He thought it was some kind of prank at first but he went off to call my GP and came back shaking his head. "I've never seen anything like this in my life," he exclaimed. "It's a miracle!"

The doctors kept me in the hospital overnight, and the next morning I had another visit from the ENT specialist and a speech therapist, who said she would help me learn to talk again. When a child first talks it has a natural instinct to breathe as it speaks, apparently, but as an adult I had forgotten this instinct. With my many years of miming practice I enunciated well enough, but I didn't *breathe* as a talking person does. After being voiceless for so long I now found myself literally choking on my words.

The first call I made on the phone was to Mum. She didn't believe it was me at first - she thought one of my friends was playing a trick on her. Then Dad took the receiver. "You sound just like an Australian," he laughed.

Now that I had my voice back, I just had to learn to control it. I soon realised that it all comes down to breathing. Without breath there's no volume. After a few days I tried to sing, but of course it was still too soon for that. I only croaked. Arguing was also out of the question, as in my agitation I would forget to breathe and nearly pass out. It took me several years before I could argue with someone, and even now, if I don't remind myself to breathe, well, I don't win many arguments.

Some weeks later, when I had completed a course of speech therapy, the specialist said I didn't need to see her anymore. She was still amazed by my case but after examining me again she didn't think I would have any complications. She looked at me as if I was some kind of spiritual being, or maybe an alien. Before she left she held both my hands and wished me luck. She said she looked forward to hearing from me in the future, and she didn't charge me for her time. She said she couldn't; it was an honour just to have helped me.

After a month of rehabilitation I returned to the DSS. My manager Daniel and my friend Rosie had already visited me at home and they'd told me that the staff had been advised to give me space, and not overwhelm me. All the same, I couldn't help myself that first day. As I passed Alan on the switchboard I finally got my own back. "Home, Home on the Range, Where the deer and the antelope play," I whispered. Alan gasped. He struggled up out of his wheelchair and grabbed me in a big bear hug. "Don't do that 'Rie, you might hurt yourself," he said. It felt like the best hug ever. Apart from it being difficult for Alan to leave his wheelchair, it was the first hug I'd ever had in the office.

The rest of the day went well enough but I don't think I did much typing. I couldn't believe how happy everyone was for me. One clerk wanted to touch me - she said I was blessed and wanted some of it to rub off on her. It *was* overwhelming. Some of my workmates even cried.

It wasn't so wonderful when the initial euphoria wore off, however. Physically, I was on the mend, but I wasn't doing so well psychologically. One minute I was angry; the next minute I was tearing up. Sometimes I was ecstatic but then I would suddenly feel depressed. The loss of my babies still wore heavily on me and I consumed a lot of paracetamol and vodka during this period.

Everyone I met would tell me how I should feel. "You must be overjoyed," was the standard reaction, but to tell the truth, I wasn't really. My world had been transfigured but I wasn't equipped to deal with it. I had recovered my voice but my emotions were all over the place. And it might sound vain, but I thought I sounded like a wounded animal when I spoke, even if no one else seemed to notice. Not wanting to appear ungrateful, though, I did my best to put on a happy face. I remembered what Nana once told me: "When someone asks how you are, the last thing they want to hear is a list of all your woes."

Rohan Greenland from the Canberra Times came to write a story about me after his girlfriend, who I worked with, told him what had happened. I was nervous at first, but Rohan said he would wait as long as he could before printing the story, to give me time to adjust. He was a nice bloke, Rohan, and he waited several weeks to print the story, just as he promised.

The Canberra Times finally printed the article in December 1984. Rohan decided not to print a photo with the story as he knew that I wouldn't want strangers to recognise and harrass me. But my anonymity didn't last long anyway. I hadn't thought the general public would be that interested, but as soon as the Canberra Times article came out I was inundated with requests for interviews on TV and radio.

The DSS was really good about it all. They let all the TV reporters and camera crews in to do their interviews and they never once gave me a hard time about it. It was exhausting, talking with all the journalists, but they pretty much already knew what they wanted me to say. Christmas was just around the corner and everyone wanted a story with a happy ending, so that's what I gave them.

Most of the reporters were respectful but one journalist asked really stupid questions, like if I make any noises when having sex, or if I talked in my sleep. He wanted to know if I had any proof that I couldn't talk for all those years. Jesus Christ, I thought - just ask around!

Anyway, one Thursday I was working late and this particular journalist broke into the building, wanting a one-on-one interview. I don't know how he did it but I guess he got through the door when one of the staff members left for the day. I remember that I was typing away when my phone rang. It was an internal call so I picked up the receiver, and it was him. He said it would be easier if I just told him which floor I was on, otherwise he would go floor by floor, room by room until he found me.

I still had Rohan's number, so I went into Daniel's office and called him straight away. The Canberra Times was just around the corner from the DSS, and Rohan said he would come to get me. He told me to wait two minutes and then to run down the fire stairs and out the emergency exit.

Those two minutes seemed to last forever, but I did as Rohan said and ran down the fire stairs and out of the emergency exit. Sure enough, Rohan's car was idling on the side of the road. A couple of his friends were standing by the car, and one of them held the passenger door open for me. I threw myself inside and Rohan drove off immediately.

As we took off down the road, I looked back and saw the journalist rushing out of the building, just as I had done seconds before. Then Rohan's friends walked towards him, and I saw him put his hands up as if to say "easy, guys." That's the last I saw of him. Maybe they all went to the pub for a beer? With them all being reporters I'm sure they'd have had plenty to talk about...

In the weeks after my story came out I received flowers, letters and cards from all over the world. Europe, England, America; every one of them was positive. Some people wrote about how they suddenly believed in God because I was a 'walking f...ing miracle', as one woman put it. Another epistle commanded me to use the gift I had been given to help others. Jesus, no pressure, guys!

In any case, now that I no longer had to laboriously mime or write my thoughts down, communicating became a whole lot easier. And, after all these years, I could finally use the telephone again. For real.

By mid 1985 I had been talking for about nine months and progressing well, even if I said so myself. When I went back to see the speech therapist, she was surprised at how quickly I'd picked everything up. She thought it was because I had been miming words all those years when I couldn't speak. Top marks to Sister Teresa who first made me mime in the school choir. It seemed so stupid at the time, but I guess it paid off in the end.

Despite recovering my voice, however, I still had problems with breathing and talking at the same time. If I was upset, excited, or angry, I would forget to breathe and I'd get the 'dizzies'. A few of my mates thought it was funny to antagonise me until I almost passed out, but they stopped when they realised that it actually hurt me. The dizzies weren't very nice. If I felt stressed when I talked I would start gasping and then I would become muddled. I could still hear noises around me but not the actual words being said. I would feel pain between my shoulders and it could take a few minutes for my body to regulate itself.

In those days I used to practice talking by chatting with shop assistants. The fact that I could ask for what I wanted now, rather than just pointing and taking whatever they gave me, was in itself amazing to me. But it wasn't just the shopping - I could talk to anyone and everyone, even strangers on the bus or the street. Despite the difficulties, it was liberating to be able to finally voice an opinion, to actually say what I was thinking.

I could carry a proper conversation, at last. Even being able to answer someone in another room was a delight. Previously I'd had to physically go to the person if they weren't standing in front of me.

Sometimes I'd get up, forgetting for a moment that I could speak, but then I would sit back down and clear my throat to call out. That felt good. But the other thing I would forget was that people *could* actually hear me. I had to be careful not to say stupid things out loud. Words had a habit of just falling out of my mouth in those days, and I would get caught out. It still happens sometimes, to be honest.

CHAPTER 23

Time continued to pass, as it always does, and as my voice slowly grew stronger my life resumed a kind of normality. Neil and I got back together and eventually had two wonderful daughters, but I could never forget the babies I had lost, and I carried a persistent sadness which deepened further after Dad died of lung cancer. Over the years we moved up to Queensland and later to Tasmania and then back to Sydney, but wherever we went I felt troubled. I felt that something was missing, although I didn't know what it was or how to find it. By the early nineteen nineties I hadn't given much thought to God for almost a decade, so it was quite a surprise when I found myself back at His door, at the Narrabeen Baptist Church.

It was one of those grey Sundays. The clouds were skidding heavily across the sky, too fast for rain. It might have been the anxiety that I felt on leaving home, but it was as though electricity was crackling in the air; as though lightning was just waiting to strike.

My intention that day had been to move back to Warilla for good. Neil and I had been fighting, and I had packed the car with essentials and taken off with the girls. But in my haste I took a wrong turn at an intersection and got hopelessly lost as I tried to get back on the highway. Somehow I ended up in a suburban cul-de-sac, unable to turn around because of the dozens of cars parked there. I turned the engine off and glanced up, wondering when the storm would break. But it must have already passed us by, because the clouds were thinning and slowing in the sky. Just then the sun pierced through from above and I noticed the sign on the building ahead: 'Narrabeen Baptist Church'. People were heading inside and I didn't think too much of it at first. Oh well, I thought, we'll just stay here until after their service and then we'll head off when I can turn the car around.

All of a sudden there was a knock on my window and a woman asked if I needed any help. I explained to her that I had just taken a wrong turn. "Come in with me," she smiled. "I'll introduce you to Anne and we can get you and the children a cold drink - it's going to get hot out here." Her voice was soft and low, but the strange thing is that I don't remember what she looked like, and I don't remember ever seeing her again after that day.

Anne turned out to be the wife of Noel Edwardes, the pastor of the church. She was kind and sincere and after meeting her I found myself sitting in on the service that day. I was a little worried by the fact that she was the pastor's wife, but I soon learned that it didn't matter to Noel where I came from or what I had done in the past. He was happy to meet me as I was in the present. I felt so welcomed by them both that the girls and I stayed on after the service, and from that fateful day forwards, Noel and Anne helped restore both my faith and my self esteem - they were true Christians.

In retrospect I can't help but believe that God brought me back to His house that day. The community at the Narrabeen Baptist Church were nothing but loving and caring, and from the first moment I met the congregation I felt that I could just be myself, without fear of judgement. Being accepted like this, without question, was as if a huge weight had been lifted from my soul. I wondered if I should tell Noel and Anne about the coven, but Noel said that God already knew everything anyway. On the one occasion I did relay some of my experiences, Anne didn't blink an eyelid; she just listened. After I talked we prayed together and I felt my spirit lighten in a way that I hadn't known since before losing my first two babies, years earlier. I felt that I was where I was supposed to be. I felt free and safe and no longer scared of my own shadow, as I had been for so long. I didn't understand exactly how this good fortune had come about, but I vowed to make the most of it.

With Anne's encouragement, I became involved with the 'Know Your Bible' classes that were hosted at Narrabeen Baptist. The 'open discussions' at KYB could get very animated, as the classes were non-denominational and there were attendees from a number of churches. It was always interesting to listen to each others' 'church traditions', and I came to understand that the most important aspects of our faith were the aspects that we all agreed on. No matter where we come from, I realised, our differences are always outweighed by what we have in common.

I was like a sponge with those bible studies, and I felt completely at home with the women at KYB. No one criticised each other, and no subject was taboo. There was no such thing as a 'stupid' question, and nothing was 'irrelevant'. That's what the classes were for: to learn as much as we could about the bible and the history and culture of the Christian faith.

The more I became involved, the more I gained an appreciation for interpretation. Rather than trying to see everything in terms of black and white or right and wrong, I learned to accept that different people can have different perspectives - many of the passages in the bible are very 'grey', after all.

Without a doubt, Narrabeen Baptist Church was the most generous congregation I have ever come across. Not just in terms of sharing what they had, but also in generosity of spirit. The community that Noel and Anne had fostered through NBC was one of patience, tolerance and kindness. Everyone accepted each other just as they were, quirks and all. It was the perfect place for me.

One Sunday I was standing with Anne and a few other friends at the back of the church, as I still could not bring myself to sit up the front. As stupid as it sounds, I was still afraid of God seeing me. After one of the hymns Anne turned to me. "Why don't you join the choir, Marie," she said. "You have a lovely voice." I was flattered but I didn't have much confidence. "Oh, I couldn't," I replied. "I can't hold a tune and I can't keep up all the time, either." But Anne said it didn't matter. "You have a nice tone," she assured me. "You should come along on Tuesday night."

My speech was getting better and better, but in those days I regularly got what I call the 'hiccups', and my voice would sometimes just drop out for no reason at all. I tried to weigh up my fear of embarrassment against my love of singing - I still had difficulty balancing my voice and my breath but the chance of joining the choir in the church that I loved was like a dream come true.

After thinking it through I came to the conclusion that if I joined the choir, the practice and training might help rehabilitate my voice. But making a decision and following through on that decision can be two different things. Singing softly at the back of the church I could manage, but standing up there at the front, before the whole congregation? That was something else entirely. In the end I stressed so much about whether or not to take up Anne's offer that I nearly made myself sick. Even after I drove to the church that Tuesday evening, I still sat in the car deliberating. Finally I couldn't stand it anymore and I bit the proverbial bullet. What the hell, I thought. If it doesn't work out I won't go back, but at least I will have tried. I took a deep breath and walked in, before I had time to change my mind.

The choir accepted me with open arms, of course. They were all so easy going that my fears melted away as soon as I joined them. I warned Rod, the choir leader, that I couldn't hold a tune for long, but he didn't seem concerned at all. "That's why you're in a choir," he said. "No one has to do a solo if they don't want to." So that was it. From then on every Tuesday night was choir night.

Tuesday night soon became my favourite night of the week. After dinner, I'd drive over to NBC for choir practice. We would all arrive around the same time; a queue of cars driving into the cul-de-sac. The church at Narrabeen, like other Baptist churches, was really just a hall. It didn't have the grandeur of crucifixes or holy statues, so it was easy to mingle and talk, or in our case sing, without feeling overwhelmed. The atmosphere was always relaxed. We goofed around and carried on, but we took our singing seriously, especially when Rod stood in front of us with 'that look'. He didn't need to say anything; he would just stand there like a chastising parent. It was all in his eyes. 'Now, now, kids, play time's over - let's get on with it,' his eyes seemed to say, and we would all fall into line. Rod had good ears too, and he knew exactly which songs would suit each of us. Jess and Joy were our sopranos, so they usually performed any solos that were called for. I would have loved to be able to sing like them, so effortlessly - their voices just poured out of them like honey.

I wasn't one to be picky, but one of my least favourite songs was the Hallelujah Chorus. We sang it at Christmas, but I could never get the words in the right order. If you've ever tried to sing it, you'll know what I mean - it's really difficult. I used to count the Hallelujahs on my fingers, but I still got it wrong, and the fact that we all sang in parts didn't help. It was too easy to follow the person next to me or behind me, rather than sticking to my own part. One of the guys, Jermaine, would poke me in the back when my part came up, but rather than prompt me, it give me the giggles. I think it was Harry Secombe who once said he couldn't sing opera because he would always laugh - it sounds weird but I think I know what he meant.

I practiced a lot but I was still apprehensive the first time I sang in public with the choir. My worst fear was that I would forget to breathe and would pass out. That would be like throwing up when I was given communion as a child. The thought made me shudder but it didn't happen in the end; we breezed through the performance. I don't even remember seeing the people in the congregation that day - I guess I was lost in the moment.

I sometimes accompanied Larry, Noel's associate pastor, on his weekly visits to the nursing homes around the parish. Larry had a poodle that went everywhere with him. Everyone loved this poodle, especially my daughter Melanie, who ran up the aisle of the church after one Sunday service yelling "Larry, marry me... Marry me Larry, I want the 'ploodle'!"

Larry loved music too, and he helped us organise NBC's Christmas plays. But he was from the USA so he always wanted us to be more 'animated' with our singing. He was used to his congregation back home being more outgoing than we were. "Put some life into it, guys," he said, in his mid-western drawl. "This is a joyous occasion. The congregation don't want to see corpses on stage!" I couldn't help myself - the thought of zombies on stage gave me the giggles all the way through that night's rehearsal.

My friends in the choir were forgiving of me even before they knew my history. Whenever I lost the tune or forgot where I was in the song, they would cover for me and help me find my place again. For my part, I knew my singing didn't meet the standards of the pop stars I adored, but I was bursting with the sheer joy of just being able to sing, after all those years of voicelessness. To be able to make any sound at all was a blessing. And then to be able to manipulate that sound and to lift my voice into song - it was as if I was finally returning from the wilderness.

In those days I was always looking for new ways to extend my vocal skills. Rod taught me how to harness my 'head voice' and then I learned to master a stronger sound by breathing from the diaphragm. I still wasn't that great a singer, but even when my voice sometimes failed me without warning, I was in heaven just being in the choir, doing what I loved.

I was so into it that I would practice singing literally anywhere and everywhere. I would sing in the car; I would sing in the bath; I would even sing while shopping in Woollies. I was doing just that one day, singing up and down the supermarket aisles, when a deep velvety voice came over the tannoy: "That wouldn't be one of my singers, practising the Christmas songs down there, would it?" I almost fainted before I realised it wasn't divine intervention - it was pastor Noel's voice. He and Anne had happened to be doing their own shopping in the supermarket that day, and when he heard me singing Noel had asked the manager to let him use the intercom. It was a good prank, but it took ages for my poor heart to stop racing. I guess I knew that it couldn't really have been God above speaking to me, but after so many years of being mute I still sometimes forgot that my voice could be heard, and I hadn't even realised I had been singing out loud.

In December 1994 we were practising for our Christmas play, when lo and behold, a reporter from the Manly Daily called me. Somehow he had come across my story from ten years ago, and he wanted to do a follow up. "Pretty please," he asked. "It's such a feel-good Christmas story." Oh well, I supposed. It wouldn't do any harm. I agreed to meet him to answer a few questions and have my photo taken.

That following week my story was everywhere again - all over the media. This time it was a little less stressful as the major newspapers syndicated the story from the Manly Daily, so I didn't have to talk to each of them individually. But there was still radio and TV. After the first few interviews it was all a bit of a blur, to be honest. When Alan Jones gave me a call for a live chat on his talkback show, I didn't even realise who he was until after I'd hung up. Come to think of it, maybe that was a good thing.

Our Nativity play was a sell-out at NBC that Christmas. There were so many people queuing outside that we had to put on extra sessions. My friends in the choir were very amused by all the attention. Jermaine nudged me backstage. "Why did you never tell us your story?" he asked, shaking his head. "Well, it didn't have a happy ending until now," I grinned.

When the curtains opened all we could see were people packed wall to wall and bright colours sparkling everywhere. We had set the stage up as a lounge room with a huge Christmas tree to one side, and as the music started we each hung an ornament on the tree and placed a present underneath it. Then we hugged each other as if we were all part of a big family get together.

Mum and Denise smiled up from the front row and I said a little prayer for Dad, and for Nana as well.

I thought about the strange journey of life that had taken me from one side of the world to the other; to voicelessness and back again. I thought about all the friends who had helped me in small ways or big ways when so many forces seemed to conspire against me. I considered all those that had maligned me or done me wrong over the years, and I made a resolution to forgive them. If there was anything that finding my voice taught me, it is that life is for living in the moment, not for holding on to past woes and resentments.

As we sang our songs that night I did my best to project the pure joy that I felt, being able to sing after so many years of silence. I wanted more than anything to share that joy, not just with my friends in the choir and the audience in the room, but with the whole world. I think we got the Christmas message well and truly across that year.

CHAPTER 24

"Everything in life happens for a reason," Nana used to say. Well, that may be true at some higher level, but down here in reality I certainly have not been able to make sense of the ups and downs of my life as I have been on them. It can be hard to see 'reason' in life, and sometimes I believe we are simply not meant to. Most of the time we are too caught up in the moment to be able to step back and see the big picture anyway - it's usually only in the context of hindsight that we ascribe meaning to life's events.

It may be stating the obvious, but times have changed since Nana's day. Back in Bolton I was brought up to believe in God and the saints, and during my childhood everything revolved around the Church - it was the backbone of society. The nuns baked bread, and they sewed and knitted clothing for the more unfortunate in the community. We, the children, would be given parcels to deliver after school to the poorest families who lived near us. There was nothing unusual about this; it was just the culture that I grew up in.

I guess it's natural to view our childhoods through rose tinted lenses, but the nuns and priests I knew during my primary school years in England were genuinely good people. We were taught to respect them - to never answer them back or to refuse when they asked you to do something - but they didn't abuse their positions; they led by example. And at the same time they were still human. It wasn't unusual to find the parish priest on a

Saturday afternoon at the football, or later in the pub, having a drink with the rest of the town.

I was taught that God is all-seeing and that the church is His house. So I was always well- behaved in church as a child, because I was sure he was watching me. I remember being asked to fetch a candle from church for one of the nuns; I couldn't do it - I thought it was stealing and that 'He' would know. The nun laughed when I told her, but that was literally what I believed. I imagined God to be the proverbial old man with a long beard and a big stick, keeping an eye on us all, ready to beat down anyone who sinned.

When I lost my voice and Father Moran and the sisters at St Anne's told me that God was punishing me, I couldn't help but partly believe them. I know now that it was conditioning, but even though I knew I hadn't done anything wrong at the time, I still felt guilty. Throughout everything that I went through, my fear of God persisted. By fear I don't mean 'respect', but real Fear, with a capital F. I've always found it hard to reconcile this 'Fearsome God' with the 'loving father' image that the new testament portrays. I think that's why I latched onto the figure of Jesus, as an archetypal 'brother' figure. I could relate more to the image of the caring young man that Jesus was, rather than to the angry old figure of authority that was 'God'. Maybe it's because I never had a brother of my own, but I thought of Jesus as a sort of 'big brother' - one that you can go to when you've pranged the car or something; you ask him to help fix things before 'Dad' finds out.

After my experiences at St Anne's, I really felt as if I were excommunicated. Even though other men of the cloth were kind to me, I was convinced that God hated me and that I had no place as a Christian. I still talked to the Jehovah's Witnesses or Mormons who came knocking at the door, but it took me a long time before I attended any services. I remained very much afraid of Catholic churches, as the buildings alone sent a wave of nausea through me. With time and effort, however, I managed to look in on a few of the more 'casual' denominations, and each December I would brace myself for Christmas Mass with Mum.

When I eventually recovered my voice I was still something of a rebel. On the rare occasions that I went to Church, I would question everything the minister sermoned. At the time, I figured that this wasn't such a bad thing if it made me more aware of what is actually written in the Bible, but the trouble was that the Bible didn't always make sense to me. I would lookup passages in the various books to see if what had been preached was 'right', but I would often just end up confused.

In my adult years I continued to doubt the relevance of God in my life. While I was living in Tasmania there was a 'revival' that I was tempted to go to, but I got cold feet at the gate. It was too soon, I realised. I still carried a lot of self-loathing with me. I felt I wasn't good or kind or loving enough to be part of a congregation.

Up in Sydney's northern beaches I went to a Pentecostal church in Dee Why a few times, but I didn't feel right there either. The Pentecostal church reminded me too much of the Spiritualist Church, and I had come to view spiritualism as my 'crossing of the line' - the step that started my journey to the 'dark side' with the coven.

When I found Narrabeen Baptist it was as if I had finally found the Church that I was looking for. Pastor Noel and his flock were loving and accepting in the true Christian sense, and the 'Know Your Bible' sessions that I attended helped me gain a better understanding of my faith. For three years there I was part of a community that saw God and the world in the way that I wanted God and the world to be. I will always be grateful for my time with them and for their belief in me.

If the whole world was like the Narrabeen Baptist community it would be a much better place, but the truth is that NBC is just one small group of people. When Mum's health began to fail I moved back to Lake Illawarra to be closer to her, and I realised that it's the people themselves that are the key. I missed Noel and Anne and the NBC community all the more when I attended the Warilla Baptist Church. The feelings that I had felt so strongly in Narrabeen just couldn't be replicated.

These days I go to Church when I wish and if I feel compelled. Some of my Christian friends say that we need each other for spiritual support, but I have found that I am more suited to flying solo. I still attend congregations now and then, but life has taught me that I am generally better off keeping my own counsel.

Not everyone appreciates this attitude. Even while working on this book I have received threatening phone calls and letters, and have been approached on the street by people wanting to 'help' me. One lady said I had a 'Spirit of Infirmity' attached to me. She claimed that this spirit keeps making me sick and she said I needed her to pray for me. I'm sorry, I thought, as she went on and on, but am I missing something here? Every illness I have had, from cancer to lupus, has actually happened in a weirdly timely manner. I have always recovered from one illness *before* I have contracted another. Rather than God punishing me, that could be God protecting me, for all anyone knows. I appreciate the intention of wanting to help, but there can be a fine line between piety and sanctimony.

Looking back on everything, the question of forgiveness naturally comes up, but to be honest I think it's something that is easier to say than do. It makes me think of a girl I know, who was assaulted. This girl was counselled to forgive and forget, all that stuff. But when I talked with her I realised it was actually impossible for her to forgive her assailant. And she felt even worse, being told to do something that she simply could not do. "I can't forgive that man for what he did," she told me. "I think I'll hate him forever."

I related to her sentiments. Why should she forgive the man who assaulted her? Yes, you need to get on with life and not let hatred and all those negative emotions overcome you, but on the other hand they are entirely normal feelings to have when you've been hurt. There's no benefit to telling yourself that you must forgive, if you are not ready to forgive. And as for forgetting...

My personal view is that anyone who has experienced trauma should be encouraged to acknowledge their feelings, and shouldn't be pressured into 'forgiving and forgetting'. Curl up in a ball in bed if you need to - there's no shame in that. Rage against the iniquities of life. But the next day, or maybe the day after that, or at some point in time when you feel that you can, pick yourself up and do something. I guess that's pretty much the advice that Nana gave me as a child, but it's worked for me, despite how much the world has changed since her day. And it might sound trite, but I've found that time really does heal all wounds. Eventually. If you let it.

One day not so long ago I was at a function where I came across Sister St Patrick from St Anne's. It was a surreal experience, but I didn't feel the need to exact revenge like I always thought I would. She wasn't even the same person she had been back at St Anne's; she had grown old and life had taken its toll on her body and her mind. When I introduced myself she seemed genuinely to have no recollection of me at all. In that moment I realised that while I might always resent what she had done and who she had been, I couldn't bring myself to hate the frail old woman in front of me. So is that forgiveness? I think sometimes, as humans, it might be the best we can do.

'God' for me has mellowed these days. He doesn't chase me with a big stick (or tennis racquet) anymore, and rather than waiting around every corner to punish me for my transgressions, He hovers somewhere in the background, behind and above me. He is more of a 'force' in my life than a 'being'.

"But do you still *believe*," I get asked, "after everything that happened to you?" My answer is yes, I believe in God. The truth is that I always have believed, even in my darkest days. I *believe* in Him because I *want* to believe, and because my faith gives me a meaningful framework within which to understand my rollercoaster life. It took me a long time to find some sense of peace with God, but I have come to realise that He did not cause any of of my troubles. Men and women were responsible for all that. But then I have also met men and women that have supported me or believed in me without any benefit to themselves, simply out of the kindness of their hearts.

Thinking back to Nana, 'everything happens for a reason' is not an adage I take literally. It's just one of those expressions people take comfort from, like 'God moves in mysterious ways'. These sayings are more about attitude than 'truth'; more about accepting the unexpected than actually understanding why things happen. That's fine, but it can be frustrating when people turn them into platitudes. I prefer a more pragmatic point of view. I think you just do the best you can, especially when you have no control over the big picture.

I've long since given up on trying to work out why I have been subject to such ill will and also such generosity in my life, but I guess there's no way to truly measure or compare these things. Maybe I would not have been able to appreciate the good things if I had not suffered the bad? Perhaps the trials and tribulations that I have experienced were in some way necessary to the journey of my soul? Certainly the experiences I've had have made me the person I am. If I had experienced a different life then it stands to reason that I would be a different person. I can't say what that person would make of me, but I hope that they would see someone who lives for the goodness in life. I hope that they would know that I wish them well and that I respect any differences we may have.

EPILOGUE

I was voiceless for my entire young adult life. Communication is paramount to relationships at any time, but as a teenager it was devastating not to be able to have normal conversations. Writing is so much slower than talking, and there is much that is lost without the inflection or tone or the rhythm of speech. I relied on short, sometimes abrupt sentences which didn't always put across exactly what I was trying to say.

My greatest regret is that I wasn't able to talk with my parents for all those years. I regret all the things left unsaid because they took too much time to write down. Mum could lip read very well, but sometimes even she could not understand me, especially if I was upset. Now that Mum and Dad are gone I can't help but wish I could have made more of our time together.

Being mute for so long taught me a lot about the way people behave. I learned that some people can be cruel when they don't understand a situation. And that can be very hard to take, especially for a young girl. It has a lasting effect. Even since recovering my voice I can't disagree or argue without getting stressed and struggling to breathe. And I still have nightmares sometimes, of drowning or of being in a bad place and not being able to call out for help. But nowadays I can go into my dreams and tell myself that it's okay, it's just a dream.

I really do believe that music saved me during my darkest days and that miming along to the songs I cherished helped me get through. Maybe my singing was 'better' when I couldn't be heard but that doesn't concern me. The greatest joy of regaining my voice is being able to sing, so I guess my story is more about the love of *having* a voice, rather than about having a 'great' voice. Even now I sing when I'm happy, and I still sing to overcome nerves, or when I'm angry or upset. I have special songs for different circumstances, but whether it be a familiar favourite or something new by one of the young pop stars that my daughters follow, I am always at my happiest when a song is in the air.

These days I'm a proud grandmother of a gorgeous little boy and girl, and I work as a medical secretary in Wollongong. Writing this book has brought me back into contact with the Elvis girls and other old friends for whom I'll always be grateful, and I have been reminded not only of the times when I thought everyone and everything was against me, but also of the small mercies and little miracles that helped me when I least expected them.

So life goes on, I guess. Looking back might be a cathartic, or a nostalgic or a painful process, but maybe its value can best be measured by how it helps us live in the present and look forward to the future. Even if I can't say what may or may not be in store for me, I can say I'm at peace with who I am and I know I'll be okay, no matter what. Whatever I may yet have to face, I'll look between and beyond the challenges to the good things ahead. After all, I still haven't forgotten Kurt Russell and that kiss under the Southern Cross...

1959 Australian threepence coin

The original coin on my bracelet.

O'Toole family 1950s (from left):

Front row: George & Mary Schofield (nee: O'Toole), Betty Burke, Nana: Molly O'Toole (Burke), Mum: Veronica O'Toole, Dad: Danny Orr, Charlie Burke.

Back row: Joe Burke, Joan & Eddie O'Toole, Francis O'Toole.

One of the rare photos I have of me in school uniform. I didn't like having my photo taken back then.

My old school badge.

Picture of me and the girls (Melanie and Danielle) at Narrabeen Baptist Church Christmas Special.

Dear Maria,

What a lovely Christmas gift and a surprise for you.

Also a Christmas gift to the people of Australia and the world, to share the joy of such a glorious happening with you

Have a happy Christmas and a perfect New Year

- Yours sincerely,

Vivie S. Hill.

A letter I received from a lady in the USA, after I started speaking again.

If you are thinking about suicide or experiencing anxiety, depression, or a personal crisis, help is available. No one needs to face their problems alone.

Beyond Blue provides information and support to help everyone in Australia achieve their best possible mental health, whatever their age and wherever they live.

Call **1300 22 4636**
Available 24 hours a day / 7 days a week

Lifeline provides all Australians experiencing a personal crisis with access to 24-hour crisis support and suicide prevention services.

Call **13 11 44**
Available 24 hours a day

Printed in Great
Britain
by Amazon